ZEN
SEEING,
ZEN
DRAWING

ZEN SEEING, ZEN DRAWING

MEDITATION IN ACTION

FREDERICK FRANCK

BANTAM BOOKS
NEW YORK · TORONTO · LONDON · SYDNEY · AUCKLAND

ZEN SEEING, ZEN DRAWING
A Bantam Book / May 1993

Book Design by Chris Welch

Library of Congress Cataloging-in-Publication Data

Franck, Frederick, 1909–
Zen seeing, Zen drawing : meditation in action / Frederick Franck.
p.   cm.
ISBN 0-553-37146-0
1. Franck, Frederick, 1909–   . 2. Painting, Zen.   3. Zen
Buddhism.   I. Title.
NC139.F72A4   1993
741'.092 — dc20

92-32791
CIP

Published simultaneously in the United States and Canada

Bantam Books are published by Bantam Books, a division
of Bantam Doubleday Dell Publishing Group, Inc. Its trademark, con-
sisting of the words "Bantam Books" and the portrayal of a rooster, is
Registered in U.S. Patent and Trademark Office and in other coun-
tries. Marca Registrada. Bantam Books, 1540 Broadway, New York,
New York 10036.

PRINTED IN THE UNITED STATES OF AMERICA

To the artist-within
EveryOne and to
Claske, who after
all these years is
still happy when I
draw.
And to Leslie Meredith,
my inspiring editor.

CONTENTS

The Meaning of Life is to see.
—*Hui Neng, seventh century*

I have lived through two world wars, survived miraculously the horrors of this cruel century, and yet . . . my eye always has been in love with the splendors of the world that surround us. My response to what I see has been to draw, and the more I have drawn the greater has become my delight in seeing and my wonder at the great gift of being able to see. I only have to stop drawing for a week to feel my eye go dim, to feel starved and impoverished. And so I draw everything—leaves, plants, clouds, swarms of birds, humans in the street. One day I realized suddenly that the seeing and the drawing had fused into one single undivided act. I called it seeing/drawing. It was a revelation, and it changed my life.

While I had at that point been drawing and painting for many years, and had had lots of exhibitions, the revelation of seeing/drawing turned upside down all my views on art and on what it means to be an artist. Being an artist does not mean covering clean pieces of paper or canvas with ink or pigment. It does not mean solo exhibitions or prizes. It definitely does not mean labeling ourselves "an artist." When I hear someone proclaim: "I am an artist," something in me whispers, "That so?" But if they say: "I paint," or "I draw," or "I play the piano," I like to talk about painting, drawing, or playing the piano with them. Saying, "I paint" or "I am a painter or a pianist" may be a factual statement, but "artist" is an honorific. Proclaiming oneself to be an artist is all too pretentious. Art is neither a profession nor a hobby. Art is a Way of being.

The artist-within, the only authentic one, however repressed and distorted, is for real. The artist-within does not indulge in self-labeling; the artist-within has no pretensions.

I could not keep the momentous discovery of seeing/drawing and the artist-within to myself. Seeing/drawing is not something apart from my life, it is my way of being in total contact with life within and around me. Having discovered the artist-within me, I began to see the artist-within others, sometimes hidden within others, the human core of EveryOne. The artist-within does not just *look at* things and loving beings, the artist-within has the capacity to *see*. I began to jot down notes on this phenomenon, and the notes became a book, *The Zen of Seeing*.

After the book was published, I was astonished by the number of letters and requests I received to give workshops on seeing/drawing. Over the past twenty years I have given a few hundred of these workshops. Each one has remained an adventure, as fresh as the first. Each workshop has underscored that seeing/drawing is at least as much about seeing firsthand — and not merely looking-at — as it is about drawing. Merely *looking-at* the world around us is immensely different from *seeing* it. Any cat or crocodile can look-at things and beings, but only we humans have the capacity to see. Although many of us, under the ceaseless bombardment of photographic and electronic imagery that we experience daily, have lost that gift of seeing, we can learn it anew, and learn to retrieve again and again the act of seeing things for the first time, each time we look-at them.

And so my workshops on seeing/drawing as meditation became retreats, retreats from all the looking-at we do. They are oases in time in which the art of seeing can be retrieved. These workshop-retreats are conducted in the silence needed for seeing. For you can look at things while talking or with a radio going full blast, but you can *see* only when the chatter stops.

These workshops are very straightforward, uncomplicated affairs. From early morning to late in the day, we draw the simplest, most commonplace things of nature, the things we have looked-at all our lives, that we may have eaten all our lives but have never really seen: a cabbage, a scallion, an apple whole and bitten into, a bowl of cherries, leaves unfolding and shriveled and dried out.

Once we start to draw, all of a sudden we begin to see again. Were we blind? How could we have ignored the beauty, the intricacies of these "simplest things," the convoluted network of veins in an oak leaf, the graceful curve of a clover's stem, the starry splendor of a humble dandelion, the voluptuous curves of a green pepper? How could we have missed the ardor of that little twig wresting itself free from its mother branch? In the course of a few hours the capacity for wonder is restored, with new awe for the gift of seeing we had forgotten.

In those few hours we reconnect with nature and thereby reconnect with ourselves while seeing, while drawing. We even begin to have an inkling of what seeing/drawing might be. It is more than drawing pictures; it is a meditation-in-action on That Which Matters, a veritable breakthrough, an awakening from the years of nonseeing, from the coma of looking-at to firsthand seeing. It is as if the innocent eye of childhood is reawakened through the unjaded eye of the artist-within.

One of my students wrote me that "seeing/drawing helps pull out what is deep inside. The four-year-old in me grew up again in an afternoon."

Among the hundreds of letters I received during those years, from people who had taken part in these Zen of Seeing retreats and

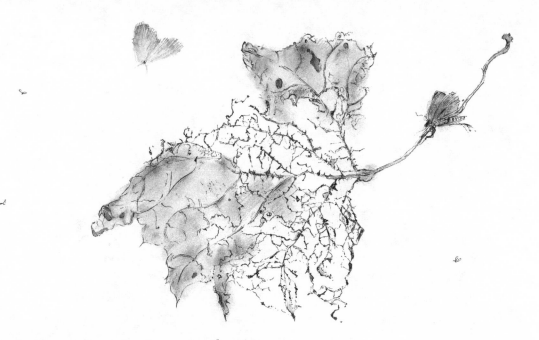

also from readers who had started to practice seeing/drawing on their own, who needed advice or encouragement or who longed to share their experiencing, there was one that differed: It said:

> I have read every one of your books. They are precious to me, not because I learned so much from them that was new to me, but because they reminded me again and again of what I somehow know, but constantly forget.

I replied: "Your letter came at precisely the right moment, for I just started to write another such reminder for you."

At the time I wrote *The Zen of Seeing*, I thought I knew about all there was to know about seeing/drawing. But then, two years ago, it was in Japan, something totally unexpected and unpredictable happened. I can only describe it as a sudden leap, a mutation in my own way of seeing/drawing. It shook me up enough that I canceled some workshops to which I was already committed and let mail accumulate unopened. I had to come to terms with this mutation. It also set me off writing *Zen Seeing, Zen Drawing*.

Again and inevitably, this book is about the process of seeing versus looking-at, of learning to see again. And of course, it is about drawing, as the intensifier of firsthand seeing, as a catalyst of awareness that makes us independent of our serfdom to technology.

When the eye wakes up to see again, it suddenly stops taking anything for granted. The thing I draw, be it leaf, rosebush, woman, or child, is no longer a thing, no longer my "object" over and against which I am the supercilious "subject." The split is healed. When I am drawing leaf or caterpillar or human face, it is at once de-thingified. I say yes to its existence. By drawing it, I dignify it, I declare it worthy of total attention, as worthy of attention as I am myself, for sheer existence is the awesome mystery and miracle we share.

I add as many drawings to what I am writing as will fit these pages, especially those drawings done after the revelation in Japan. Most are reproduced in their actual size, torn from those little drawing pads that allow me to draw in the streets, cafés, Japanese temples, Italian churches without attracting anyone's attention. Not that I consider each one a masterpiece, but I trust that what words cannot convey, the drawings will. Words can weasel and betray meaning and truth. These drawings can't. They are as direct, as nakedly truthful as the movement of the hand that obediently notes down what the eye perceives. Seeing/drawing is also about life, about life in its fullness, about learning to see again and thereby be totally alive and fully aware.

ZEN
SEEING,
ZEN
DRAWING

1

THE ARTIST-
WITHIN

The Buddha is quoted as saying: "We do not learn by experience, but by our capacity for experience."

I appeal to this capacity for experience, our capacity to see instead of to look-at. This capacity is the essence of the artist-within.

Who is this artist-within? The French essayist Charles Augustin Sainte-Beuve wrote, a century ago: "With everyone born human, a poet — an artist — is born, who dies young and who is survived by an adult."

A contemporary thinker, Rudolf Arnheim, concluded that "every child entering grade school in this country embarks on a

Upper East Side. New York

twelve-to-twenty-year apprenticeship in aesthetic alienation. Eyes they still have, but see they do no more."

Two much more ancient quotations belong here, for they touch the very heart of the matter. The first one dates back to seventh-century China, when Hui Neng, the Zen sage, said: *"The Meaning of Life is to see."*

Not to look-at, mind you, but to *see*!

Another of these ancient Chinese, Hui Hai, reminded his contemporaries: *"Your treasure house is within; it contains all you'll ever need."* This bears repeating amidst the din of television commercials for all the trivial things we don't need!

The aesthetic estrangement that both Arnheim and Sainte-Beuve deplored is not confined to people trained in engineering, business management, or computer programming. It also affects those who attend art schools, for the eye is likely to be programmed until it is benumbed, saturated with the fads, fashions, and slogans of the moment. Students may start out their art training at the prompting of the artist-within, but in the process this artist-within is browbeaten into submission, into suspended animation: "Eyes they still have, but see they can no more."

The glaring contrast between seeing and looking-at the world around us is immense; it is fateful. Everything in our society seems to conspire against our inborn human gift of seeing. We have become addicted to merely looking-at things and beings. The more we regress from seeing to looking-at the world — through the ever-more-perfected machinery of viewfinders, TV tubes, VCRs,

microscopes, spectroscopes, stereoscopes — the less we see. The less we see, the more numbed we become to the joy and the pain of being alive, and the further estranged we become from ourselves and all others.

If we could still really see what day after day is shown on the six o'clock news, we would burst out in tears. We would pray, or kneel, or perhaps make the sign of the cross over that screen in an impotent gesture of exorcising such evil, such insanity. But there we sit, programmed as we are to look-at, to stare passively at those burning tanks, those animals choking in oil spills. We perfunctorily shake our heads, take another sip of our drink, and stare at the manic commercials until the thing switches back to smiling bigwigs reviewing honor guards, rows of corpses, and beauty queens preening.

No wonder that once the art of seeing is lost, Meaning is lost, and all life itself seems ever more meaningless: "They know not what they do, for they do not see what they look-at."

"Not seeing what they look-at" may well be the root cause of the frightful suffering that we humans inflict on one another, on animals, on Earth herself.

Seeing/drawing is an immunization against the addiction to looking-at: it restores the gift of seeing — that is: of Being, of being fully alive. "I have a newborn hope to see/draw and to *live again,*" says one of the letters I got.

Hᴏᴡ ᴅɪᴅ ɪ discover this seeing/drawing, in which the seeing and the drawing fuse into one undivided act, in which eye and hand, body and soul are no longer split?

It happened around 1960 — on the equator. I was serving as an oral surgeon on the staff of Albert Schweitzer's legendary jungle hospital in Lambarene. Before leaving New York, I had vowed to use my time in Africa to get into as close a contact with Africa and Africans as possible. I had brought two good cameras.

Soon, however, clicking the shutter, even a thousand times, did not satisfy me. The machine separated my eye from the reality it perceived. People in the leprosy section of the hospital would hide

baby consultation, Schweitzer Hospital

their disfigured bodies and flee approaching camera-toters, but they sat for me as models, they felt that the act of drawing reverenced, dignified them. I locked away my cameras and, glad I had packed my drawing gear, started to scribble down whatever struck my eye. Almost at once the very quality of my perception changed. Nothing interfered now between my eye and what it saw. Every dot, every line on the paper had gone through my whole organism. I was no longer the onlooker; I had crawled under Africa's skin. Drawing the landscape, I "became" that landscape, felt unseparated from it. I "became" an African as I drew an African, often my patient. This is what seeing/drawing really does: You become what you draw. Unless you become it, you cannot draw it.

Later, drawing in Japan, in Italy, I have felt myself "becoming" totally Japanese, totally Italian — unseparated from what I drew.

It occurred to me that what I had retrieved in Africa was actually the original impulse that had made me take up a pencil and draw when I was still very young. It was my pure delight in seeing, in seeing the cloud castles sailing over the hills, the light sweeping over the meadows around my hometown in southern Holland, the peasant women selling cabbages and leeks in the market square.

My eye was in love! I had to celebrate this love and so . . . I drew. The local painters were my idols. I saw them as beings far superior to the merchants, politicians, lawyers, doctors of our provincial city — I myself became a doctor only by family pressure. These artists too were grownups, but they were the grownups who could still see! Their eye was still in love! Like mine!

Chinatown, New York

THE REVELATION OF seeing/drawing on the equator was the beginning of my defection from the New York art world, from the need for yearly exhibitions on Fifty-seventh Street or Madison Avenue. I had strayed into this gallery world a few decades earlier. Once in it, it is almost impossible not to become contaminated by ambition, competitiveness, and fear: the ambition of a museum purchase, anxiety about not getting a review or getting a bad one, of falling by the wayside.

The experience of seeing/drawing showed me that art has very little to do with the fabrication of products, of gallery merchandise, that art is not a drag race between avant-gardes with bets placed on the winner. Art is the most profound, most irrepressible response to life itself, whether that art is drawing, dancing, playing a flute, or acting on a stage. Seeing/drawing is, for me, that response. It is the response of the artist-within.

If one's art does not rise up from the deepest recesses of one's being, it risks being not art but kitsch. Kitsch — it is all too easily overlooked — may be either Low Kitsch or High Kitsch. A gondola of gold plastic that jingles *"O sole mio"* is obviously Low Kitsch. But an artifact of high technical sophistication, skill, and ingenuity, applauded by the art popes of the day, may still be kitsch — of the High variety. How do we distinguish kitsch from art? By not "looking-at" it from the conditioned head, but by "seeing it, from the belly," as Orientals would say, trusting one's intuition, one's gut feeling for what is beamed from heart to heart and not from one narcissistic ego, that of the maker, to the other, that of the dealer, consumer, critic.

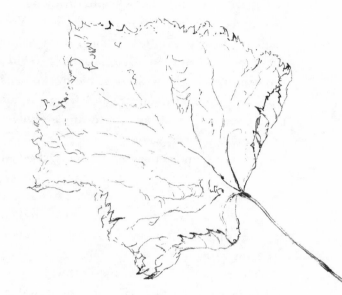

WHEN, ON THE equator, I coined the term *seeing/drawing*, I felt that I had discovered something momentous by which the lost art of seeing was retrieved and intensified, the eye deprogrammed, the artist-within — the only authentic one — literally resuscitated from suspended animation. It is not an "expansion" of consciousness but its intensification. After a while it began to dawn on me that this seeing/drawing was not — as I had blithely assumed — my stroke of genius at all! I had only rediscovered it, had hit on something that was far from new. It was venerably old! The artist-within was literally as old as . . . being human.

"How old is the Buddha?" a master once asked one of his monks. The answer he accepted was: "As old as I am, Master." "Fine," said the master, "and how old are you?" "As old as the Buddha, Master," said the monk. This applies exactly to the artist-within: He is as old as I am and I am as old as he, and that is older than old, it is prehistoric.

The seeing/drawing I had rediscovered in Africa had been invented at least as early as thirty thousand years ago, when our Cro-Magnon forebears started to draw those splendid bulls on the

rock walls of their caves in southern France and northern Spain. It was a crucial moment in the biography of our species and of the planet itself. The artist-within manifested himself in the grottoes of Altamira and Lascaux.

Ludwig von Bertalanffy, the renowned systems scientist, wrote: "It is the capacity to symbolize that is the divine spark which differentiates the most primitive human being from the most highly organized animal." And Jacob Bronowski in *The Ascent of Man* recognized this divine spark when he wrote of these first symbolizers, "Their cave drawings proclaim beyond all doubt: Man was here!"

The artist-within is not a figment of the imagination.

The implications are mind-boggling: What distinguishes us from the "highest organized animal," what stamps our Cro-Magnon forebears as the early exemplars of a fully human species,

is their art! They are exemplars not only of the fully human but of the artist-within! The two seem inextricably interlaced.

If Hui Neng is right, and the Meaning of Life is to see, these "most primitive" of human beings who had the capacity to see, to symbolize, to draw such masterpieces, must also have had some first, yet very poignant breakthroughs of insight into life's Meaning.

No Cro-Magnon ever took part in my workshops (I took theirs!), but I have seen the breakthrough to brand-new insight again and again when *seeing* starts. Suddenly all the confused, impotent scrawling stops, and the hand, synchronized with the eye, begins to draw.

But something even more astonishing seems to be correlated with this suddenly retrieved capacity to draw: It is an awakening, a new openness for and insight into the livingness of living things, a reborn capacity for empathy, wonder, and reverence, for awe for the simplest things of nature, for a leaf, a scallion. It may be momentary, but it could also be a lasting awakening from the coma of aesthetic alienation, a liberation from the conditioning that makes the adult in us survive the corpse of Sainte-Beuve's short-lived poet. It is this experience of breakthrough to the artist-within that is the theme of many of the letters I receive:

And then you looked at the leaf I had drawn. You said, "That's it, that is the breakthrough! Who taught you?" I answered, "I taught it to myself." "Hm!" you said. "Just don't think now that you are a genius, but go on drawing. Go home and draw everything, everything!"

And that is what I am still doing.

One day I was drawing a cow in a meadow near our house. As I stood there drawing, our eyes met, and at that instant she stopped being "a cow." She had become this singular fellow being whose warm breath mixed with my own in the cold fall air. We were standing eye to eye. Who, what was looking from her eye into mine, from mine into hers? Her big moist eye shifted. Slowly she turned around. My pen followed.

When I checked what had appeared on my paper, it struck me forcefully that what I had drawn was nothing other than the subject matter that had inspired my Neolithic forebears when they drew such bovines on the walls of their cavernous living rooms. I was back at the cradle of the artist-within EveryOne!

Something in me had jumped back to a moment before history began, had freed me from all of history's permutations, swept aside all of Greek, medieval, Renaissance, and modern art, dismissed all the influences of all those generations of artists that preceded ours and conditioned our seeing. It was as if they had never happened! I had drawn this sister cow directly "from life"! I had drawn life as this eye-of-my-own had perceived it! I had leaped back thirty centuries to the very Origins.

When the Ten Thousand Things are seen
in their Oneness
we return to the Origins
where we have always been

Seng-T'San

One can paint *à la* Matisse, *à la* Miró, *à la* Pollock, even — if extremely gifted — *à la* Rubens. Seeing/drawing taught me that however hard you try, you cannot draw *à la* anyone but yourself. You can only draw the perception of this eye-of-your-own. A

Picasso who could annex so brilliantly any style of painting he fancied, became in drawing the Cro-Magnon who must draw what his eye perceived, albeit in his own unique handwriting.

Even "technically," this primeval response to life has remained almost unchanged during these thirty thousand years. All it still requires is a surface to draw on, a simple tool to draw with, and the innocence of the human eye as it once was, before it was conditioned by school, church, or an art course, or as it is once more when its innocence is retrieved and all its programming, its aesthetic alienation is overcome.

For when I am not drawing, driving my car, or stopping at a traffic light or a bus stop, in a park, my eye continues to register a face, a body bending, a pattern of trees swaying in the breeze. Nothing is lost.

As I continued to draw whatever happened to come into my field of vision, it became ever clearer that seeing/drawing was indeed a Way, in the Oriental sense of the word. The tea ceremony, Noh dance, aikido, judo (*do* in Japanese means "Way," while in Chinese the word for Way is *Tao*) are all such Ways: lifelong disciplines that lead you to where you really live, that liberate you from the programmed prejudices of your time and the pretensions of the little Me, to reveal the truth that is your own Truth. Seeing/drawing proved to be a mode of that "Way of seeing" of which the sages of the East have spoken over the centuries: a Way of meditation, of prayer if you will, for those whose temperaments, like mine, are all too active, too Western perhaps, for long hours of sitting motionless in meditation. It is my Way, but then there are as many Ways as there are human beings.

It is my Way of meditation. The eyes not closed, but as wide open as possible! It might be your Way.

It is as simple a Way as one might wish for. It consists of allowing the eye to be fully awake to life as it presents itself, uninterruptedly, in its myriad manifestations: the subtle variations in the forms of five little pears on your table, a bird gathering sprigs of grass to build its nest, a woman pushing her baby carriage on a country lane at dusk.

Apart from this constant mobilization of the eye, all that is needed is a little sketch pad in your pocket and a pencil or pen, and to let the hand follow — whether brilliantly, or awkwardly at first — what the eye perceives, and to keep on doing this with eyes and mind and heart wide awake. Epiphany of the commonplace.

2

A NOTE ON SEEING/ DRAWING AS ZEN PRACTICE

In this book I speak of Zen as I understand it — if *understand* is the word — and as I practice it. When half a century ago I first encountered Zen in the writings of Daisetz T. Suzuki (1870–1968), the sage who almost single-handedly initiated the West into the world of Zen, I was overwhelmed. I felt as if I had been parachuted into a landscape in which I had never set foot, but where at once I recognized every hillock, every tree, every tuft of grass. I knew at once that Zen was not some intellectual or philosophical system, that it was not a religion, either, but a religious orientation to life as such, an orientation that must be an essential ingredient of all religions, beyond their beliefs, theologies, myths,

and precepts. I felt at ease with the statement that Zen could not be "taught" but could only be transmitted from heart to heart. Zen, after all, is indeed: to be in direct touch with the innermost workings of life inside and at the same time around oneself. It is as useless to hold forth about Zen as it is to prattle about art: both Zen and art have to be experienced, they have to be practiced.

The practice of Zen is normally described in terms of sitting in the objectless meditation known as *zazen*. In one of the branches of Zen, Soto, *zazen* is the very crux of this practice. In the other, the Rinzai branch, *zazen* is supplemented by the concentration on koans (*ko-an*). A koan is an enigmatic statement that the Zen master gives to his disciple to contemplate and to "solve" but that the intellect is powerless to deal with. One has to *become* this enigma, this koan, which is not a logical proposition but the expression of a state of mind interwoven with the Zen discipline. By the disciples' attempts to solve the riddle, the master can judge their spiritual progress. The endpoint of this preoccupation with the koan is the full realization of the Truth that is the Ground the disciple shares with his teacher: The very Meaning of Life is touched through this device. This turnabout at the base is known as *satori*, usually translated as "enlightenment." I wonder, however, if "awakening" is not more adequate, for it is the awakening to the intimate contact with the Sanity at our core.

Seeing/drawing is my way of practicing Zen. Fundamentalist Zennists may scoff at this and question its validity as Zen practice. I myself had some doubts, until many years ago a revered Zen

master, Abbot Kobori Nanrei in Kyoto, reassured me completely. He confirmed that seeing/drawing was obviously *my* Way of practicing Zen, an artist's Way.

Seeing/drawing, my meditation by eye and hand as one, has never become a routine. When I start a drawing, I have no inkling of what the outcome will be. Just as every single one of my workshops is a "first," so is every drawing my "first." I'll never be a "professional," I am a perennial beginner.

From D. T. Suzuki, I learned that every art has its mystery, its spiritual rhythm, its *myo* in Japanese. The *myo* is intimately related to all the arts. The true artist, the artist-within, is the one who is really moved by the *myo*, the as-is-ness of things, of their intrinsic, unhallowed sacredness.

When I draw a tuft of grass, a face, a crowd, I am confronting this as-is-ness of things, their *myo*. It is not *behind* their appearances, for these appearances are more than skin-deep. The appearance of things is the manifestation of the *myo*, of their Meaning, for those who have eyes to see: "The Meaning of Life is to *see*."

WHEN A MASTER was asked, "What is the Tao?" he answered, "It is right in front of your nose!" The monk protested, "So why can't I see it?" "Your Me is in the way," the master answered.

Zen is the breakthrough from the Me to that True Self, which is also known as the Buddha Nature, as the True Man without rank (or attributes) in this hulk of red flesh, as the Indwelling Spirit.

Hui Neng's expression for this Specifically Human in us — hence for the artist hidden within — is: "The face you already had before you were born, before even your parents were born, your Original Face."

ANOTHER MASTER, WHEN asked, "Who were the sages who taught the Buddha?" answered, "The dog and the cat." Zen masters don't explain, but I presume that this means that as dogs have their dog nature and cats have their specific cat nature, so we humans have our specifically, genetically human nature, which is our "Original Face," from before birth.

The Buddha is for me the manifestation of that Specifically Human Original Face, and so is the Christ: pure paradigms of our humanness. For me, "I am before Abraham was" refers to the Original Face, and so does "I and My Father — Truth/Reality — are not-two, they are One."

There is too much flippant talk about killing the ego, destroying it, as the precondition for that Zen awakening to our essential Sanity, to our quintessential Humanness.

I believe that there is a semantic error at work, that ego does not have to be destroyed but must be expanded until it embraces all: "What you do to the least of these, you do to Me." The Me in this saying is not the little Me, the ego encapsulated in its bag of skin. It is the ego liberated from its isolation and infinitely, cosmically extended. All the boundaries between I and Thou, between subject and object, have been crossed, erased.

I and other humans
no difference.
     Ikkyu (15th century)

What I and all other humans, and indeed all other living things, have in common is *impermanence*.

The thirteenth-century Zen master Dogen defined Buddha Nature as being impermanence. We do not just *have* the Buddha Nature, according to Dogen; we *are* the Buddha Nature.

When things are seen in their fleetingness, their impermanence, not only is the Great Wisdom born, but so is that other pillar of Buddhist insight, the Great Compassion, that impartial love that may include one's enemy and that in Christian terms is indicated as *agape*. This Great Wisdom/Compassion is bound to spring up from the realization of the Mystery, the sacred mother lode from which all looms up, of which all is made, to which all must return.

Z EN RESISTS DEFINITION. I have only tried to point at it as: *Life that knows it is living and must die.* Seeing/drawing is the constant confrontation with it. Seeing/drawing the cow, I am confronted not with cattle, with livestock, not even with "a" cow, but with this one unrepeatable cow. Drawing a crowd, it is never fixed for a second. It is in uninterrupted change, yet each one in this crowd is not only "just" as she/he is but also most definitely "such" as he/she is.

The Tao lies before my eyes.

Meister Eckhart, the fourteenth-century Western, Christian, Zen man, said: "When is a man in mere understanding? When he sees things as separated one from the other. And when is he beyond mere understanding? When he sees all in all."

Albert Schweitzer wrote, "Mysticism occurs whenever a human being sees the separation between the natural and the supernatural, between the temporal and the eternal, as overcome." Zen, which is less mysticism than a radical realism, would smile gently: "Isn't the natural supernatural enough?" For Zen rejects all such dualisms.

The last word in this little note belongs to Hui Neng, for he is the seventh-century father of Zen as it is still very much alive today: "The wisdom of the past, present and future Buddhas is immanent in our own mind. If we cannot enlighten ourselves, we have to seek the guidance of pious and learned masters. Those, however, who can enlighten themselves, don't need such extraneous help. Why? Because of our innate wisdom through which we can liberate ourselves."

"The Kingdom is within and without you," says the Gospel according to Thomas. So is Hell, Zen would add.

It depends whether you see, or merely look-at things.

Paradise is at your own center
unless you find it there
there is no way to enter.
                    Angelus Silesius

3

THE
REFLEX
ARC

Seeing/drawing is neither "modern" nor outdated. "Modern" became outdated when "postmodern" bric-a-brac became the fashion. Seeing/drawing is timeless.

Every authentic artist has rediscovered seeing/drawing anew, has practiced it, from the Greek vase painters, to Leonardo, Michelangelo, and Rembrandt, all the way to Delacroix, Degas, Klimt, and Schiele. Their every scribble proves it.

THE CRUCIAL EVENT in Japan that made me start writing this book was preceded by a deeper grasp of the process of seeing/drawing as it came to me in my long practice and experience of it,

and also as I observed it evolve in the many workshop-retreats I have given.

Sometimes the impulse to draw overwhelms me all of a sudden, as it did on a day on a crowded street in downtown New York, when I saw an old fellow approaching. He was the one person in that dense crowd who struck my eye, so that after I passed him, I was compelled to turn around on my heels to see him limping toward me once more. I had not looked-at the man, for then his image on my retina would have been signaled from my eye to the computer in the skull that would have processed it as: "male, sixtyish, white, poor, limping, decrepit."

But I had not looked-at him, I had *seen* him: I did not process his image in my computer-brain, as I would have for a police report. Something very different had happened.

When his image hit my eye, the reflex arc was set into motion in which the image on the retina ran — still unlabeled — from the eye through my entire organism, through the arm to the hand that held the pen that traced a graph on the paper. When it came to a stop, the graph was the drawing of this particular man limping on his cane.

By now, I knew this man. I had "become" him, had been a child with him, a cocksure adolescent. I had grown old, worn out with him. His feet were killing me. . . .

The graph traced by the pen has become like that of a seismograph. The pen became the seismographic needle that registers the slightest tremors on my retina. This did not come about overnight.

On the contrary, it was the result of endless practice in coordinating eye and hand, of jotting down whatever I saw. There is no trick to it, there are no shortcuts. There are no manuals for sale on how to draw old fellows limping toward you. You just go on drawing. For every drawing is your latest exercise in the fine-tuned coordination of eye and hand, ever more sensitively, ever more truthfully.

These endless exercises, however, are neither a boring routine, nor are they repetitious or mechanical. Each one is a keen experiencing, an intensification of your awareness, each one enriches your life, adds to its fullness, deepens your perception of the commonplace as Mystery.

At one moment it is a leaf drifting down, announcing Fall's arrival, at another it is a child skipping rope. Here it was this

particular oldster in the dense anonymous crowd who struck my eye irresistibly, compelled the hand to start moving, made my entire nervous system leap into a state of tension from optic nerve to fingertips. All choosing, planning, thinking, stopped. What the seismographic pen traced was this graph, this little drawing among so many, pretenseless products of the process of seeing/drawing; exercise!

*The Great Way is not difficult
just avoid choosing*

Sen-T'sang

All development in seeing/drawing consists in the ever greater sensitization of the reflex arc, of the pen responding to the truth of seeing. I simplified my description a bit by leaving out one crucial detail: The nonstop flight of the image goes from eye to hand — via the heart.

If this should raise an eyebrow, *heart* does not refer here to the pump in the chest. It is what the ancient Chinese called *hsin*. *Hsin* denotes both "heart" and "mind." The Japanese too have one single word, *kokoro*, for this mind/heart, the spiritual core, our "soul." Mind/heart, *hsin*, *kokoro* is involved in the reflex of seeing/drawing, intensifying consciousness to the utmost. That leaf I drew has gone through the *kokoro*. It has become precious to me. I hesitate to throw it away. It is the *kokoro* that brings the drawing to life, that transmits its spirit to the one who views it. The drawing becomes the communication from heart to heart, from *kokoro* to *kokoro*. Art is a function of the *kokoro*.

"The *kokoro* is the Buddha, the Awakened One. Apart from *kokoro*, no Buddha," said a medieval master.

In Holland, in Belgium, I draw the landscape of my childhood where seeing began for me. Here I fell in love with that hill! The beloved high poplar I had to hug is still there!

In Verona, drawing on the Piazza Bra, I feel as Italian as any Veronese. In Padua, drawing Paduans at their noon conference, I feel I have known each one forever. The clerics I draw in Parma still scare me as they used to do long ago in my Dutch hometown.

Am I "expressing" these Paduans, Veronese, and Parmesans? Or am I "expressing myself"? Neither! I let them express themselves through the reflex, the little Me free-wheeling.

And yet what I have drawn is stored forever in the "treasure house within," in the *kokoro*.

The critical contrast between seeing and looking-at cannot be overestimated. Seeing touches the *hsin*, the heart. Looking-at is cold-hearted. The difference may be a matter of life and death.

The Good Samaritan helped the mugged man not after consulting his code of ethics or phoning his therapist for advice. He got off

his bike because he happened to *see* the wretch lying in the road. The image in his eye that rushed nonstop via the heart, the *kokoro,* made him save a life.

To see is our Original Nature, our True Nature. To look-at is a product of our conditioning. To see is not to grasp a thing, a being, but to be grasped by it.

Is there anyone who reads this who does not recall being coldly looked-at, that is, pigeonholed as a "this" or a "that," dismissed as too ugly, too thin, too coarse, too fat, too knock-kneed, or too white, black, or yellow, who did not cry out deep inside: "Please, don't stand there looking at me! Can't you *see* me?"

To *see* is that specifically human capacity that opens one up to empathy, to compassion with all that lives and dies.

Oh, kill it not
see how it wrings
its hands, its feet
the fly.
    Issa (1769–1826)

As I am writing this, a leaf comes drifting down and lands at my feet. It is a withered leaf, yellowed, cankered, shriveled, curled, as leaves are in late August. It is as-it-is.

As Chuang Tzu in 500 B.C. knew a fish's joy in the river by walking along the river, I became that leaf, and as I drew it, it became my self-portrait.

"Tat Twam Asi, That Art Thou," says an Upanishad. Whatever you draw becomes self-portrait; leaves, girls, old men.

The Buddha on a walk with his disciples picked up a leaf and said: "This leaf represents all I ever taught. Now, monks, watch all the other leaves, they represent what I have left unsaid." I would have taken my pencil and drawn some of the other leaves, a young one, a shriveled old one.

When I am drawing a tree, an apple tree for instance, I may break off a twig with a few leaves and draw it first, to get into intimate touch with the life pattern of that tree. Drawing this detail discloses the inner structure, the Suchness of that apple tree. In my workshops, I always have an array of leaves to offer: young vital ones, wounded ones, last year's dried-up leaves, musty, curled-up dead ones. Each one in itself is an inimitable parable of the process of appearing and disappearing, of being born, of growing, being blown about, fading, and dying. We practice really seeing these leaves by seeing/drawing them, their veins and inner structure, their edges and stems. We notice their uniqueness, their being-as-they-are.

I believe that I keep on giving my workshops in seeing/drawing because of the joy that witnessing the breakthrough of the artist-within gives me. That moment remains ever new. The looking-at stops, the seeing starts, and lo! they can draw!

This breakthrough happens to people who have not drawn since fourth grade, as it does to professionals, to art teachers, and to designers. What astonishes me every time is how despite all their years of aesthetic alienation, this breakthrough often needs no more than my gentle little push, a push to see through our habitual images of things, to see afresh. What this little push consists of is still mysterious to me, but it must have something to do with the longing, the inner drive that makes a person join my workshop and to which I respond intuitively, totally.

When I am asked, "What is your teaching method?" I answer therefore truthfully: "I do not teach and have no method." These workshop-retreats are based on my unshakable trust, or faith, in the seer, the artist-within everyone, hidden and repressed by conditioning as they may be. It is not my task to teach but to liberate this artist-within, to deprogram the eye from looking-at to first-hand seeing.

All I can do is to stimulate that awakening by pointing-at, by focusing the full attention on what the eye perceives, to let the hand that holds the pencil follow it, until the moment comes when I feel as if I were a mother hen who, hearing the chick pecking at the eggshell from the inside, must respond by pecking from the outside until the shell breaks. At this moment, the artist-within breaks through from conditioned looking-at to seeing/drawing.

Perhaps I could paraphrase Bodhidharma, the sage who brought Zen from India to China fifteen hundred years ago, to explain this breakthrough. He said that Zen is the transmission of That Which Matters, outside of all the words of scriptures and philosophies, and pointing directly, heart to heart, at the human *kokoro,* restoring our contact with our True Nature, whether spoken of as the True Self, the Buddha Nature, or the Indwelling Spirit. Hui Neng called it the "Original Face we had before we were even born." What else could it be but that which is most Specifically Human in us, what else but the artist-within?

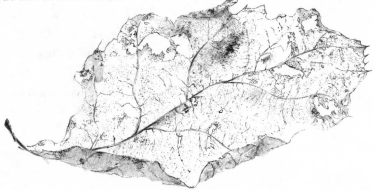

43

Often the letters I get from workshop participants recall that moment of breaking through the shell. One of these came from Ohio, where I had handed an oak leaf to a young man as his first assignment. He started to draw. Wildly nervous scrawls covered sheet after sheet that had no connection with that leaf or anything else in nature. This is not unusual at the beginning of these retreats, so I waited patiently for his agitation to quiet down. It did not. For hours on end he kept scrawling incoherent scribbles. I became a bit desperate. Was Ohio going to be my Waterloo? I went out on the lawn, picked a little weed some four inches high with a tiny white flower at the top, and put it on his drawing pad. "Try this," I said. At last he was making contact. The scrawling stopped, and the little weed started to grow on his paper. Suddenly he stopped.

"What is the matter?" I asked.

He looked upset and pointed at his model: "It is already wilting!"

"So it is, just go on." He did.

A little later I noticed he had stopped again. He sat bent over his paper. Was he crying?

"Look! It is *dead*!" he whispered in horror.

"Draw it dead, as-it-is," I said. It became a touching drawing. He wrote:

I thought, I have killed millions of them with my lawn mower and never gave it a thought. I still mow my lawn, but now I know what I am doing. . . . You bet I am still drawing!

*Of an early death
showing no sign
the cicada sings.*
Bashō

The Ohio story may seem sentimental. To me it is not. It became a parable of what happens in the breakthrough, in the awakening of the eye from looking-at to seeing, of the reawakening of the Specifically Human, of the artist-within. Is it not this Specific Humanness awakened that is irreconcilable with letting children starve to death and torturing people in basements?

*The one awakened
liberated
sees all things as one
unseparated.*
Angelus Silesius

4

INTERMEZZO ON HOW-TO AND HOW-NOT-TO

Some of the letters I have received from students and readers say things like:

> For years I was afraid to pick up a pencil. I so needed this workshop to break through the fear. . . . For the first time I drew peacefully instead of feeling competitive.

And another:

> I have been teaching art for many years. This workshop started me on the road to understanding in a different way what art is

about. . . . You exorcised some demons surviving from my art school training and made me confront the habit of nonseeing.

But this one was decisive:

I had grown fearful of drawing. My enjoyment was nil. Now that phobia has been dispelled and I'll go on and on. Thousand thanks.

How many there must be out there, fearful to pick up a pencil, afraid of not being able to "draw a straight line"—as if nature abounded in straight lines—intimidated and confused by all the pontifications of art columns and the jargon of coffee-table art books, by museums presenting the abstruse as if it were the Ineffable.

After having declared that I have no "teaching method" and that my workshops rest on nothing but direct, intuitive contact, "heart to heart," it is paradoxical to try to convey in words how seeing/drawing begins. And yet I want to give in a few pages a brief view of the basic form of my workshop, which, combined with what I write here about my own experience, I hope will be helpful to the reader for beginning to see and draw. For I do believe that neither "technique" nor "talent" matters half as much as the deconditioning of the eye from looking-at to seeing. The moment firsthand seeing is retrieved—and I have seen this confirmed hundreds of times—the hand starts to move in obedience to the eye and finds its own "technique," which only constant practice will refine, enrich, and enhance.

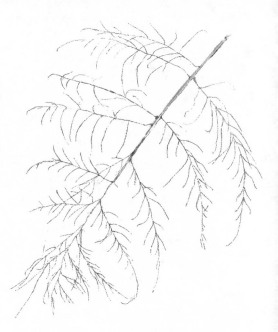

THE WORKSHOP

The equipment you need could not be simpler. It consists of a pad of smooth, white drawing paper, about 12 by 17 inches, an HB pencil — or better still, a 0.5 mm mechanical pencil with HB leads — and a kneadable eraser.

I banish charcoal and watercolor from these workshops, not because they are not splendid materials but because they give all too flattering "artistic" effects, which interfere with seeing. For today is an experiment in firsthand seeing, a seeing so intense that it and drawing can fuse into seeing/drawing. A pencil neither lies nor flatters, it simply registers "artlessly" what the eye perceives.

I limit these workshop retreats to twenty participants, for I have found that that is the maximum I can handle responsibly. Officially we start at nine in the morning, but if the group is not yet complete, those present are asked to start right away and draw something from memory, a few leaves or a tree or perhaps a leafy twig. They draw in silence, for we avoid all small talk during the workshop.

Before each workshop, I withdraw to prepare myself for what has always remained an awesome experiment, an almost scary adventure that seems a "first" even if it is the three hundredth. When I face these twenty total strangers, I must establish with each one of them — almost instantly — a profound and purely intuitive intimate contact, or else I can't be of any real help. This contact has to be so close that I must be able to see through these twenty pairs of eyes what each of them sees. But even that is not enough, for unless I can also identify with each one's inner rhythm, I might incorrectly hurry up the person who perceives and responds slowly and put the brakes on another who perceives and reacts with lightning speed and will produce thirty drawings against the former's ten or fewer. In either case, I would be forcing the person out of his or her natural orbit, would sin against precisely that authenticity to which I am committed.

When all are present, the drawing from memory stops and I can start the workshop proper with my brief introduction. It always varies, but it inevitably stresses the day's experimental, thoroughly noncompetitive character and the prime importance of maintaining silence. Looking-at can be combined with chatter and background music. Real seeing demands silence.

This day will not be devoted to "self-expression," even less to making "art objects" or "being creative." It is simply an experiment in retrieving the lost art of seeing and, I hope, an initiation into that seeing/drawing in which seeing and drawing fuse, for this seeing/drawing *is* the meditation.

Indeed, seeing/drawing is not "self-expression." When I draw this leaf, it is not I, the little Me, that is expressing either itself or that leaf. Rather, the leaf is allowed or invited to express itself by means of the eye-heart-hand reflex. Today's workshop does not pretend to be more than an initiation into what may become an ongoing process, a lifelong discipline. If I say we are not going to "be creative" today, it is because the word *creative* is by now covering all-too-wide a variety of sins. What I really mean is that at those rare moments when intense seeing turns into seeing/ drawing, we may realize ourselves to be part of that Creative Process that unfolds unceasingly in nature, in all the universe. They are those moments of grace, of which Wan Shi said a thousand years ago: "I and the Ten Thousand Things are of One Root."

It is at such moments of grace, when the looking-at stops and firsthand seeing is retrieved, that the hand begins to follow obediently what the eye perceives: Seeing/drawing has started, and the breakthrough of the artist-within has happened!

From this point on, you should let the artist-within guide you. Just continue to draw as much as you can, draw whatever strikes your eye. All that is is worthy of being drawn, and all that is discloses itself in the meditation-in-action that is seeing/drawing.

There are no groups to join, no expensive lessons to take that may merely lead you astray. Seeing/drawing, moreover, is guaranteed recession-proof. It costs nothing: A pencil and a piece of paper can always be found. Wherever you happen to be, there is a cornucopia of models, of subject matter. You will never be bored or feel lonesome, for the moment you start seeing/drawing, you will realize being a living part of a living universe. You will be in close contact with the innermost workings of life inside and around yourself. Where this contact becomes intense enough, you forget yourself, you are on the threshold of the Zen experience.

At the end of the workshop, or as I hope, at the end of this book, you may conclude that seeing/drawing has indeed been an initiation into something of real meaning, and you may perhaps embark on seeing/drawing as your Way, as an ongoing spiritual discipline that brings you ever more in touch with your quintessential Humanness, with your own Truth. Isn't this what true spirituality is about?

This, in brief, is how I introduce our workshop-retreat. We begin in attention, memory, and silence. "But there is something," I add, "that cannot be expressed in words, yet seems to be essential for me to start this day in the right spirit. It is a little ritual that is far from being artificial or trivial. We stand in a circle, and I bow, from the center, to each one in the circle and expect a bow in response. Then, holding hands, we bow to the entire group.

"What does this ritual mean? It implies absolute human respect for one another, independent of 'achievement.' It also means — to me — that whatever hesitations, failures, or shortcomings you have today, I have gone through them all, and not only many years ago: I still have to overcome them each time I pick up my pencil and start drawing."

In those few minutes of the "ritual," I am all eye. It is as if a total picture of every single one in the circle imprints itself on my inner eye. According to that imprint, I choose the first leaf I give to you as your first assignment.

AN EXERCISE

From this point on, we'll pretend I am on a house call to give you a private workshop.

Let's imagine we are sitting at your kitchen table and that I hand you this serrated leaf I picked in your front yard as your first challenge. Start to look at that leaf as intensely as you can. Open yourself up to it, take it in for four or five minutes. Notice that it is not just a flat oval thing. The slender stem becomes its main vein, and it and the secondary and tertiary veins form a system of channels, of blood vessels so to speak, through which the sap rising from the earth through the trunk of the tree, through branches and twigs, reaches this leaf to nurture it. It is far from a mere herringbone pattern — it is alive! Notice also where the leaf's edges are serrated.

Now place the leaf on your drawing pad, in the upper-left-hand corner of the paper so you don't have to focus and refocus. Look at it again for a few minutes, then close your eyes and try to visualize it in every detail while you hold your pencil loosely in your hand, its point resting on the paper.

Now open your eyes and let them focus on the leaf. You are no longer merely looking-at the leaf, you may begin to *see* it! Keeping your eyes riveted on that leaf, let the point of your pencil start to glide on the paper, and feel as if the pencil point were caressing the contours of the leaf. Don't press on your pencil; keep your hand loose, free, and slightly above the paper, and keep on "caressing" that contour. For now, it is important that you do *not* check the marks the pencil makes on the paper. This is no more than a first exercise in coordinating eye and hand. Just keep on feeling that the pencil's point is caressing that contour.

"I began to understand what caressing means," someone wrote me about this sensation.

For half an hour or more, continue to do this caressing. You will become aware that the contour with which you are in contact is not confined to the outer edge of the leaf only, but that your pencil has, almost on its own, been in touch with other, unsuspected contours that cross your leaf in all directions. Follow these internal contours as they strike you, and notice how your pencil climbs up and down hills and valleys, for that leaf is not a flat pancake but a living, billowing being.

Ah! Now you are cheating! You are checking what appears on the paper, as if that mattered in this preliminary exercise in coordinating eye and hand. How do I know you are cheating? Because if you had not checked, how would your pencil know where to connect those secondary veins to the central one? Just try again; keep drawing without looking at your drawing, just by seeing the leaf and letting your pencil move. Your drawing may or may not look like the leaf in front of you, but for this exercise, let go of your expectations of how a drawing of a leaf should look. Even if the drawing turns out not to look like the leaf, it will reflect some of the truth of the leaf, its contours and textures, its being-as-it-is.

At this point, after about a half hour of the caressing exercise, take another sheet of paper, place the leaf as before, and draw for another hour — this time let yourself check once in a while where your pencil is going. In this next drawing, the leaf is already becoming more recognizable. You can now follow the central and secondary veins and connect them to one another as they are.

You may notice capricious serrations in the edge of the leaf. You may even try to draw all these serrations, may do so almost mechanically, until those edges look like saw blades. When that

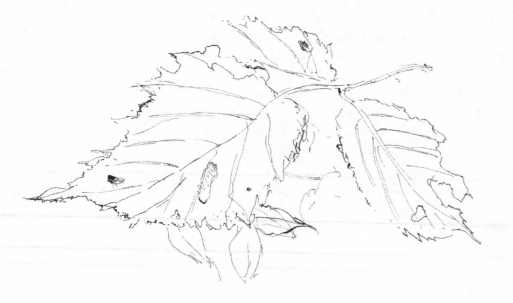

happens, it only proves that you have temporarily regressed from seeing to looking-at, for you drew serrations that you could not possibly have seen but figured ought to be there. You don't have to draw every single serration! Why? Because you can't possibly *see* them all. Only draw what you see, don't draw what you don't see or what you think *ought* to be there.

Now draw that leaf's contour once more, and notice that from where you are sitting, these serrations stand in some spots sharply contrasted with the background, while in other spots they hide in the shade. Again don't draw what you suppose to be there: your pencil should be activated only by what your eye truly perceives. We are seeing/drawing, remember? We are not tracing diagrams for a botanical textbook.

"I wonder how to draw that billowing leaf with its hills and valleys?" you ask. The answer is, there is no how-to. There is only seeing! Just follow some of those secondary veins very sensitively from where they sprout from that central vein, and let your pencil follow them from there over hills and valleys to the edge of the leaf, and lo and behold, the leaf begins to billow, the edges begin to curl where you see them curl. But you can do more, and that is our next experiment. It is an experiment in . . . squinting!

You may never have noticed it, but our seeing seems to consist of a rapid alternation between sharp focusing on an object and squinting at it through your eyelashes. If you squint for a moment, you'll notice that at some points the contour, including those serrations, stands out very sharply against the background. Here, for instance, the edge of the leaf contrasts strongly with the light background. At other points the contour practically disappears, even becomes invisible, for there is a gradual transition into the background.

Wherever you see a sharp contrast, try to press a little harder on your pencil. You see what happens? Your leaf is beginning to come to life, it seems to lift itself from the paper because of these variations in the intensity of the line. The line has become "expressive line": all by itself it expresses light and dark. It even expresses a third dimension. If you are serious about seeing/drawing, you will want to practice this hundreds or even thousands of times, for it is an essential ingredient of it, part of that meditation that consists of being in maximal contact with visual reality — in this case, that of your leaf. This contact is so intense that it is as if you had become unseparated from that leaf, that you had "become" it. It is no longer "just a leaf." It is this particular, unrepeatable leaf, as you are that particular, unrepeatable you. If you draw it again and again without letting your concentration sag, your meditation deepens further and you are in touch with the life process as it manifests itself in this humble leaf. You are "beholding the lilies of the field"; you "see how they grow." The leaf is looking back at you! The eye-heart-hand reflex has been activated!

One glance at your drawing shows me, and should prove to you, that yes, here the meditation has started. Now we are ready for the next and crucial experiment, the Dry Run.

But first a remark on something that often strikes me while I am watching my novices: the destructive tendency to go over lines again and again until they are no longer lines but a mess. This happens when one's main attention is no longer focused on what is being drawn but on what appears on the paper, and so one tries to "correct" a form without having really seen it. Not only does it prove a deficiency in real seeing, it is incompatible with making a line expressive, with making it sing. Try to let go and begin anew on another drawing if you catch yourself going over your lines too much.

THE DRY RUN

Watching people draw in my workshops I notice that sometimes they draw a leaf about three times its actual size. When I ask them if they can tell me why, they usually reply, "Oh, it just happened." It happens all the time, but it should not, unless you want it to happen. I see leaves being blown up to poster size or reduced to that of a postage stamp. I see them pushed into a corner of the paper or beyond, for no reason at all.

Let me give you a little demonstration that I have found indispensable in all my workshops for curing those afflicted with gigantism or pygmyism. I initiate them into the secrets of the Dry Run.

This Dry Run is a gesture, but far from an empty gesture. And it is more than a rite. Although I have never seen it described in any book, it is the essential prelude to whatever you draw, be it a leaf, a tree, a landscape, or your beloved.

The Dry Run consists of gesturing on the paper the place, the shape, and the size of whatever you are going to draw before you allow the pencil to come into action.

In the case of your leaf, let your finger gesture it in its actual size where you want it to be — let's say, in the center of the paper, leaving a great white emptiness around it. Or if you should decide to reduce it, gesture it at some other location on the paper, perhaps

in the upper-left-hand corner. If you plan a large mural of leaf forms, enlarge the leaf to cover all of your paper as a study, and let your finger gesture it accordingly.

But whatever you decide to do, in this Dry Run two important things are bound to happen. First, the image of what you are about to draw imprints itself on your awareness, and almost simultaneously both the position and the size of the drawing-to-be become preestablished and clarified before the pencil is used at all. Such a Dry Run takes at most a few seconds.

I am convinced that artists have used the Dry Run consciously, semiconsciously, or unconsciously from time immemorial. Its usefulness is almost too basic, too self-evident, to make a point of mentioning it. But if you start to draw a human figure without having done a quick Dry Run to place it on your paper, chances are that a shoulder will be cut off at its edge, or a foot amputated, or the head scalped. The Dry Run will prevent such involuntary mutilations. If during your finger's dance on your paper before committing yourself, a foot falls off, you simply repeat your gesturing with a bit less amplitude until the figure fits the available space you desire.

If I draw a landscape with hills, a clump of trees, a farmhouse, and a silo, I gesture in my Dry Run where the crest of the hills will be in relation to the trees, the house, and the silo, and I'll know at once where the top of the silo will be in relation to the top of the hills. Once I have let my hand dance the composition a few times across the paper, I have started to internalize the entire scene in its proportions, and I can start drawing, uninterrupted by peering, measuring, fumbling, and erasing: the landscape has been "precomposed" before I allow my pencil to make a single mark on the paper.

Now, suppose we are going to draw the still life on your kitchen table. First, let your finger gesture the landscape of plates, spoons, coffee pot, and basket of oranges. Determine where they will go in relation to one another and in relation to the available space on your paper. Only after having established this, only after the still life has imprinted itself on your awareness, take your pencil and start drawing. After that, as another preliminary exercise, let your pencil scribble down what your hand gestured, while keeping your eye strictly focused on that still life on the table. Do this again and again.

In my workshops, after the Dry Run demonstration and the exercises that precede it, minor miracles start to happen. "I felt moments of freedom to draw without self-judgment to put my soul's vision on paper. The process became timeless and trancelike," someone wrote. Indeed, the process is trancelike.

After these exercises in a workshop, since we have worked with great intensity, we stop for a silent lunch or quiet break. We maintain the silence so that the trancelike, meditative mood is not disturbed.

WE ARE READY now to confront a few of those things on your table that we have eaten all our lives, have recognized, have labeled "green pepper," "apple," "scallion," or "mushroom," but have never truly seen.

Let's start with the green pepper. A first try, after a quick Dry Run, may show your pepper as an awkward thing that looks like a half-collapsed balloon. So try one drawing and then another, for after a couple of drawings, all at once the pepper's voluptuous curves will become surprisingly convincing. Draw it in a very light

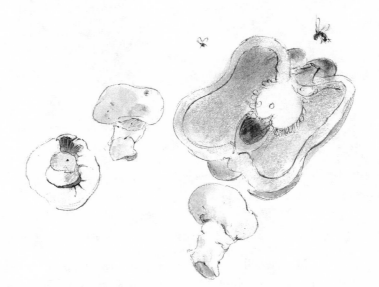

line, so that when you squint at it and see where the pepper's contour contrasts against the background, you can "accent" that light line, make it expressive of the pepper's form and volume.

Ruthlessly cutting our model in half, lay bare the pepper's innards. Draw it again in its complexity of hills, crests, and crevices, and its semicircle of seeds. It is a challenging autopsy, getting ever closer to what is *seen*, to the form, the structure, the entire anatomy of that curvaceous pepper.

NOW IT IS the apple's turn. Gesture it on your paper, exactly where you want it, in its actual size. Of course an apple is more or less ball shaped, but however hard you try, it refuses to gain its legitimate three-dimensionality; it persists in remaining somewhat of a disc. First notice that it is only "more or less" ball shaped, so let your pencil caress its contours once again very carefully in that light line, which later will give you a chance to "accent" it according to the contrasts and transitions against the background. To give the apple its roundness, there is always a strong temptation to start "shading," a euphemism for blackening. This blackening is taboo in our workshop today: It does not belong in the category of seeing/drawing but is closer to painting with a pencil. Instead of breaking the blackening taboo, squint at the apple, and become aware of how away from the light the apple's contours become almost invisible and in other places quite pronounced. Draw the apple this time in a hair-fine line. Now subtly accent and reinforce the contour where it contrasts with its background. The apple will suddenly gain its roundness—without any shading.

This little experiment confirms that where line remains of uniform thickness, the resulting contour is not a contour at all but a mere outline that imprisons a form as in an iron-wire cage. Where

line becomes expressive, however, the roundness of an apple, the volume of a thigh, comes all by itself.

In the long run, after long self-training in seeing/drawing, this accenting becomes integrated in the act of drawing, part of the eye-heart-hand reflex itself, rather than an afterthought. It is the result of the ever-progressing sensitization of the reflex arc.

OUR NEXT MODEL, of a totally different shape, is a scallion. I find in drawing scallions the beauty that is a joy forever. A scallion's long slender leaves can swing across the paper in an infinite variety of choreographies. The first try is usually a losing battle both for the novice in drawing and for the scallion. The former becomes desperate, while the latter lies sprawling on the paper in flat rigor mortis.

Still, after half a dozen or so Dry Runs — each one of which takes less than a minute — after continuing to scribble down that scallion according to the finger's preliminary dance over the paper, the scallion begins to reveal itself to be a ballerina, swinging its long svelte leaves across your sketch pad. Keep on drawing her, lightly, fluidly, and don't forget to squint at your ballerina so you can reinforce that fluid, light line where it is needed to let her dance in three dimensions.

This "accenting" is a very subtle operation of great precision, rigorously based on seeing. It is the opposite of a trick. Accenting when unjustified by seeing is an obvious fake to any sensitive eye.

THERE IS STILL time for you to slip outside and break off a leafy twig in your backyard.

Notice those umbilical points where the twig wrestles itself free from its mother branch! Along the branch itself, there are innumerable scars that are witness to abortive attempts to sprout a twig. Then, after all those vain attempts, the life-force at last succeeds and a twig is born, a twig that is not welded or glued to the branch — as it invariably looks in poor drawings. It is literally *growing* from it, so that at the spot where the life-force succeeds in its most recent impetus, there is a subtle swelling, a pregnancy. When I see this miracle clearly witnessed in a drawing, I am moved. "Here is the breakthrough, here the meditation has started!" I whisper to my student. "Wonderful, go on."

Once this miracle of growth, of life, has been seen, it will never be forgotten, it is the contact with the innermost workings of life,

with the great Mystery of Being and Becoming manifesting itself in
this little twig.

Where the twig in its turn gives birth to a leaf, the long tense
stem of that birch leaf or maple leaf is at once the supportive
connection that turns into its "backbone," the main vein. It is also
the umbilical cord of the leaf. The graceful curve of that stem will
appear in the drawing, provided you take this hint: Don't try to
give it volume right away. First draw that tense, taut curve in a
single line! Too often have I tried in vain to give such a stem its
volume from the start. The graceful line became hesitant, dented,
and the slender, elegant stem had become an uncouth gas hose.

At the end of our workshops, after hours more of drawing
mushrooms, half-peeled bananas, oranges whole and in sections,
apples halved and bitten into, I often catch people looking quiz-

zically at their drawings, especially the ones done at the end of the day. "How on earth could I do this? I hadn't drawn since fourth grade! What is the secret? And where do I go from here?" they ask.

There is no secret apart from the *seeing* retrieved. And there is nowhere to go from here but to your drawing pad. Just go on drawing; draw and draw! You will experience for yourself that all that is is worthy of being drawn: dandelion and cat, grasses, ducks in a pond, live chickens scratching, wrapped chicken corpses from the supermarket, goldfish swimming in a bowl, sardines in an opened tin. . . .

Draw whatever happens to lie on your kitchen table, and draw whoever sits down at it: your neighbor, your spouse, your friends.

"But how do I switch from drawing the still life on my table to the people sitting around it?"

Don't switch. Once again: There is no how-to! When your neighbor is sitting there, Dry Run her on your paper as if she were

a pepper or a scallion, then trust the eye-heart-hand reflex and scribble her down, keeping your eye riveted on your model. Scribble down how her body sags on the chair, how her arm rests on the table, and the slant of her head. Don't worry about proportions or likenesses! Scribble down forms without labeling them as "a nose" or "a hand" or however the other spare parts are labeled. Do this constantly, and the proportions will take care of themselves, provided you do thousands of scribbles.

Draw your own hands, your feet, and your face in the mirror, never skipping the Dry Run. Get a few friends together and draw each other. Put a small sketchbook in your pocket, and scribble down trees, landscapes, people in the street.

Maybe there is a possibility in your vicinity where you can draw from life without being confused by "instruction." I calculated that in the past forty years, I have done at least sixty thousand drawings of the naked body (I must have thrown away 55,529 of them), but I continue drawing from life, at least one night a week. Why? Because unless I keep practicing my scales, I can't play sonatas. I need this practice if I am to draw people in city streets. They are all naked under their finery — really.

Tearoom, Cologne

Two more recent letters, both from art teachers, say:

I never felt this way during my college courses in drawing and so I have not drawn much even though I teach art. . . . I feel now as if I were lifted out of a deep well.

and:

I know now what I always knew in my heart, but now it is more than knowing: instead of know-how it is the miraculous power of seeing that is to be kept fully alive and connecting.

Where art is no longer addled by the superstitions of the "art world," where it is not fame, money, or exhibitions that propel it but "connecting" with the world around you and through it with yourself, with your Self, you are free, fully alive, and lifted out of the deep well.

I know, for I have literally "drawn" myself out of that deep well. And so has another alumna of one of my workshops who, instead of a letter, sent me as a Christmas present a wonderful little handmade book about the lemon she drew. It made me very happy.

She wrote:

I felt that lemon. Its image passed from eye to hand, my brain did not mutilate it. I had cleared my mind of all preconceived notions of what a lemon looked like . . . and so I began to draw what appeared before me: a round yellow object halved by a sharp knife. I noticed its lines and textures. The simple round object now showed a complexity of lines and patterns. I drew it with heart and soul. After two hours with one single halved lemon to my credit, I showed the drawing to FF, who looked at it, muttered: "Congratulations," and added two small definite lines on the rind of the lemon "for music."

When it was time to tape some of our early and some of our later drawings on the wall, my husband had over a hundred to choose from; others tore just three or four from their sketch pads. I sheepishly withdrew, felt that my single little lemon could not compete with the talents and the productivity of the others. I did not tape it to the wall, sure that it would not be missed. I fled.

At the end of the exhibition FF spotted me: "Where is your poetic lemon?" he cried. Then everybody wanted to see my poetic lemon and I had fifteen minutes of fame.

There were many lessons to be learned that day, and not all were about art.

5

SEEING/ DRAWING IN NO-TIME

The totally unexpected mutation in my own work that spurred me to write this book happened just over a year ago, on my eleventh or twelfth trip to Japan. Japan had fascinated me visually, but it scared me. I felt inhibited in trying to draw Japan.

I consoled myself by concentrating on the Noh play, the solemn classical theater of Japan. I did hundreds of drawings of Noh. I had fallen in love with these six-hundred-year-old plays on first sight, as some forty years earlier, when I first happened on the books of D. T. Suzuki, I fell in love with Zen. For some mysterious reason, both Zen and Noh were not exotic to me at all. It was as if I had known both forever, as if they were part of me, long forgotten and suddenly retrieved.

Noh is at once sacred dance, opera, and liturgy. It is also Zen meditation as pure motion. As such I felt it to be related to the movement of the hand in seeing/drawing. It too is meditation in motion.

JAPANESE EPIPHANY

On a blustery November day, when I stood waiting on a platform of Kyoto station for the Shinkanzen, the bullet train to Tokyo, my eye was struck by three elderly Japanese. Two women were sitting on a bench, an old man on his haunches in front of them. They were eating sushi from cardboard lunchboxes. A few yards farther

away, at the kiosk, students — the boys in their black school uni-
forms, the girls in the usual navy blue sailor suits — were kidding
around, buying sodas and things to nibble. I was struck suddenly,
deeply, by this banal scene. It was as if I were watching some
miraculous supernatural pantomime. I itched to draw it, but the
train was to pull in at any moment for its precise two-minute stop.

Still, without realizing it, I must have unscrewed the cap of my drawing pen, for suddenly I felt my hand starting to move all by itself. It flew over the paper of my little sketchbook in precise synchronization with what my fascinated eye perceived. I did not have a split second to glance at what appeared on that paper. The pen kept on gliding, leaping, dancing, from the old people on the left — it even touched some little figures in the background — then jumped to the students on the right-hand page, and back.

When the train came to a stop, I hardly managed to put my pen away, grab my bag, and leap just in time. The automatic doors closed barely behind instead of in front of me. The train picked up

speed. Within seconds factories and buildings flew past, then hills and pale green rice paddies, forests of smokestacks, a thousand high-tension pylons. Still shaky, out of breath, I sat down. It took a little while before I dared to look at what that pen had thrown down in those few seconds on the paper.

It seemed impossible! How could this have happened in no-time? I was delighted but felt a bit frightened at the same time. Was I dreaming?

I sat staring at the pockmarked industrial landscape flying past, until the train began to slow down for its arrival at Nagoya station, its last two-minute stop before Tokyo. A stocky businessman in dark blue suit and striped silk tie sat down across from me, his briefcase on his knees. Japan Inc. incarnate! Before I knew it, the pen had again started its dance. I sat there staring into space, but that space contained the man the pen was scribbling down. He sat absolutely still, gazing past me, unseeing. If his eye registered anything at all, it must have been a tourist, a foreigner. If he vaguely perceived the foreigner's hand moving, he may have fancied that the *gaijin* was noting down expenses, as tourists do. Then he moved, took some papers out of his briefcase, and started to do some scribbling himself.

The train flew past a long viaduct across a wide river that looked familiar, as did the tall white building with the gigantic neon sign. We must have been quite close to Mount Fuji. I had passed Japan's sacred mountain, hidden in thick smog, at least twenty times. Today had become so bright, so sunny, that with a little luck . . .

I took a gamble, turned the page, and let my pen scribble down the people across the aisle, interfering with it only to leave some open space for Fuji in case it should decide to show itself. It did, and as we rushed past at 120 miles per hour, the mountain obligingly settled down on the page precisely in its assigned spot, in no-time. Then, on the next page Fuji drew itself once more in no-time.

Fuji

The morning mists rose
Fuji revealed itself
Ah, the day is saved.

                           Issa

Yes, it drew itself indeed in no-time. For while seeing/drawing — I had been aware of it before — time may expand and contract. A minute can contain an hour, an hour may shrink into fifteen seconds. Inner time becomes totally disconnected from linear time, clock time.

I looked at what had happened. I was definitely not dreaming. It was as clear as it was wonderful and a bit scary: All inhibitions had evaporated, as if at long last — at eighty! — I had put full trust in the eye-heart-hand reflex. I had let it do its work without meddling, without suspiciously checking whether it was doing its job properly. The reflex had simply functioned, without my interfering with it. The artist-within had taken over the controls.

The seeing/drawing that, in Africa, I had discovered to be my second nature, had become first nature. This "first nature" sat here drawing Japan from this speeding train, as if I had lived here forever. From alien territory, Japan had turned into home ground, one of my many home grounds.

Returned to Kyoto, sipping green tea in my favorite little tea garden near Kiyumizu Temple, I was watching a melancholy old couple in mid-distance. My pen scribbled them down automat-

ically, mercilessly. It added a third person in my field of vision. I was hardly involved.

A few days later, at the River Festival at Arashiyama, a whole sketchbook filled itself with flat-bottomed boats, geishas, dancers, samisen players. Once more, all at once, everything became pellucid, sharp as in a dream. Again what I was watching seemed miraculous, compelled my hand to take off. The pen danced. It danced by itself. Seeing/drawing had become autonomous, nothing but a hand that danced to the music of life. Chords, intervals, pianissimos, staccatos, fortissimos transmuted themselves into black marks of ink on white paper.

A lone white heron stood in the rapids of the Hozu River, mirroring itself in my eye. Heron, autumn dusk, rapids, and hills projected themselves onto the paper. When I looked at it that evening, I said aloud: "Ah! But this is a haiku, a wordless haiku written in lines and dots!" Since in Japanese the same verb can mean to draw and to write, I was drawing haiku—legitimately.

The old people in the tea garden, the heron, the boats of Arashiyama—in fact, all that happened on my paper since that moment on the station platform were such haiku in bits of black line, a few dots, and perhaps a quick wash of saliva rubbed in with my finger. Pure experiencing precipitated!

In Japanese, haiku are bound by strict traditional rules that do not apply in any Western language, but haiku are now also written in English, French, German, Dutch. It is more than a fad. It is the rediscovery of seeing, of celebrating the sensitivity of the eye. It converts deadly looking-at into living seeing!

The poet Masaoka Shiki wrote: "I had a flowering branch placed by my pillow. As I draw it faithfully, I feel I am gradually coming to grasp the secrets of creation." Shiki confirms what the experience of seeing/drawing had revealed to me through the years.

Bashō, the father of haiku, warned his students: "Jot down your haiku before the heat of perception cools!"

An authentic haiku must, in one breath, grasp the joy as it flies, the tear as it trickles down the cheek. In its seventeen syllables a haiku must catch the unsayable, the mystery of being and non-being: timeless mini-*satori* in fleeting time:

This dewdrop universe
just a dewdrop
and yet,
and yet . . .

                                        Issa

R. H. Blyth, the veteran translator of the entire haiku literature, agrees: "A haiku is a flash of illumination in which we enter into things."

Haiku transmit neither an idea nor a philosophy; they transmute pure experience into a minimum of words that grasp a moment of grace, be it joyous or heartrending. All that has for long seemed commonplace and dead springs at once to brand-new pulsing life. Tree, cloud, face return your glance. I see the cloud, the cloud sees me.

The great haiku poet Chiyou, an eighteenth-century woman, said, "A haiku must be the expression of inner feeling totally devoid of ego." Chiyou just could not bring herself to disentangle her bucket from the morning glory's embrace:

Ah! Morning glory
holding my bucket captive!
I must beg for water.

In the eye-heart-hand reflex of seeing/drawing the intellect, the narcissistic ego that "chooses" is in freewheel. Seeing and feeling condense themselves into the ink marks a hand jots down. To reach this point demands pointed mindfulness practiced without letup. There are no shortcuts.

When I draw the rose, it looks back at me. It contains all the secrets of Creation, as Shiki saw so clearly. Through that rose I am in touch with myself, with my Self. To be in touch with the Self, with the innermost workings of life, is what Zen is about.

Angelus Silesius, the seventeenth-century Western poet and mystic, wrote about the rose:

The rose that
with my mortal eye
I see
flowers in God for all eternity.

There is still a strong whiff of theology here, but Angelus corrected it and then he wrote the first and perhaps greatest of Western haiku:

*The rose is without why
it blossoms because it blossoms.*

This is pure Zen, and it proves the universality of Zen. As one of its greatest sages Dōgen (thirteenth century) said: "To know ego is to forget ego, to forget ego is to be illuminated by all things." Angelus Silesius, *seeing* the rose, was illuminated by it.

"The seeing have the world in common," Heraclitus had noticed a few millennia earlier. The lookers-at, the onlookers, have been killing, torturing one another ever since, are still at it.

Another saying of Bashō is: "The one who writes three to five haiku in his life is a haiku poet. Anyone who can write ten is a Master." Issa, who probably wrote more than the five hundred haiku gathered in one little book on my shelf, must have qualified with honors for his Master's degree. There is hope. . . .

I went on drawing Japan, drew the Imperial Gardens in the rain with a humble cleaning crew gathering fallen leaves under their umbrellas. I drew the gardeners of the shrine in Mamuyama Park, the market at Toji Temple, the fishmonger at Imadegawa — until Kyoto had become one of my multiple hometowns, just a little more so.

Though in Kyoto
I long for Kyoto,

Bashō wrote.

I caught myself daydreaming that I once must have been born here, long ago, in a previous incarnation — if there should be such — as a poet-monk like Ikkyu, or a great *roshi* like Daito, or perhaps even — but more unlikely — as a samurai. Gradually, my daydreams became more modest. I settled for having been a noodle vendor or a ferryman on the Kamo River.

Then, with a shock, I recognized myself, in duplicate, in the two wretched sandwichmen I stood drawing at the Shijo Bridge, which long ago had replaced the ferries.

There are countless paths
to the mountain's summit
yet from it
the same moon pours radiance
over the landscape

Ikkyu

To my immense relief I was able to take my haiku phenomenon along wherever I traveled. Hardly had I set foot on American soil when the haiku happened again. Wherever the eye mirrored people, mountains, buildings, morning glories, doves, the reflex arc sprang into autonomous action. Sometimes these haiku-in-line came in major keys, sometimes in minor. Sometimes they laughed, sometimes they smiled, and sometimes they sobbed, as haiku are apt to do.

From the tip of Buddha's nose
an icicle
                                    Issa

Skull in the grasses
all that remains
of the warriors' dreams.
                                    Buson

I flew to Europe. In the red-light district of Antwerp's harbor, the pen at once started to dance the whores and their clientele. "No comment, no moralizing!" said the pen. "They are as they are."

In the Pelikaanstraat, center of Antwerp's diamond trade, the Hasidic dealers stood gossiping, haggling, negotiating, as an entire previous generation had stood there before it was carted off to the gas chambers. Drawing these survivors, not understanding a word they were saying, I heard them proclaim what we humans make known uninterruptedly, what I have heard them broadcast in every language I understand. I have even heard it quacked by ducks, roared by lions, and clucked by chickens: I want! I like! I adore! I despise! I hate! I love! I am! We are! You ain't! They ain't!

All sins committed
in the three worlds
will fade and disappear
together with myself.
　　　　Ikkyu

On a bright Sunday morning, leaning against a wall, I stand drawing a Flemish town square. Twentieth-century people in their Sunday best are milling around against the sixteenth-century backdrop of their town hall, as alive, as merry as the transients who built that town hall had done on bright Sundays four centuries ago. They had not left a trace; nor had the ones who designed this glorious town hall and paid for it, strutted in and around it, and ruled from it.

All had disappeared without a trace, and so will the ones now milling around and the one who stands there drawing, catching the joy as it flies — and that is enough.

To what shall I compare this life of ours?
Even before I can say
it is like a lightning flash or a dewdrop
it is no more.

Sengai

True enough, Sengai! But that is not the point: Catching the dewdrop, the lightning flash is the point!

Was not Issa closer to That Which Matters when, in the seventeen syllables accorded to a haiku, he caught the unsayable mystery:

. . . just a dewdrop
and yet
and yet . . .

I took a train to catch the dewdrops. As it sped past the hills, vineyards, and castles of the Rhine, crawled up the Swiss Alps, the haiku kept coming, only to fall mute for a while in the blackness of the St. Gotthardt Tunnel. Then, as soon as we descended into Italy, the pen continued its scribble dance.

I had drawn in Verona, Padua, Venice, Rome, off and on for years, but this time, I vowed, I would leave it to the pen to do its capers all by itself. I have learned by now that whatever writes or draws a haiku, it is definitely not "artistic," "creative" little Me. It had taken me fifty years to unlearn what I once thought I knew.

On the Piazza Bra in Verona, at Saint Anthony's tomb in Padua, at the Tiber in Rome, the Grand Canal in Venice, the pen catches the natives, as it does the tourists climbing out of their air-conditioned touring cars, cameras at the ready. Five or six abreast,

they stand shooting their salvos at what they have hardly time to
look-at, let alone see. They store the potshots quickly into their
little black boxes to take home, to show at the office as proof of
their breathless peregrinations.

It draws them kneeling, Americans, Japanese, Europeans
alike, aiming their prefocused, computerized machinery in the
ritualized poses they imitate from other photographers, wrenching
their spines to hit their targets from maximally "creative" angles —
but quick! quick! for already the bus driver is hooting his horn.
The pen manages to strip them of their gaudy tourist wear before
they hurry back into their seats for the next target, tele-bazookas
in their laps.

Photographs, from Atget to Cartier Bresson, from Brassai to Walker Evans, Ansel Adams, Minor White and many others, have haunted, moved, enriched me. Still, who can deny what Walter Benjamin, a Nazi victim, wrote in one of his often-prophetic essays about compulsive snapshooting and about the frightening side effect it has of extinguishing memory. Memory is benumbed by the pseudomemory of the snapshot that catches on film no more than the looked-at fragments of an incoherent world in its meaninglessness.

Only what is really seen, experienced, lived becomes part of the Treasure House. "I shoot, therefore I am" tolls the death knell of the artist-within.

Seeing/drawing is the antithesis of this snapshooting. The whole person is committed. Far from being a hobby, it is a total openness to that which meets the eye. It is: to be in touch with the Ground of Being, inside and outside of oneself.

As soon as a drawing is finished, I see at once whether it succeeded or failed. There are no excuses, no self-deceptions. The beauty of seeing/drawing is that you are your own most unflattering critic, your own graphologist who points immediately, gently but mercilessly, at the cleverest hidden trick, the slightest narcissism, at every pretense, shortcut, cliché. No tricks are accepted. The drawing succeeds where the eye has retrieved its original gift, its openness, its innocence, and the hand follows it without questioning. As soon as it is interfered with by "choosing," by "will" — the will to fame, to profit, the will to power — it fails.

Hence seeing/drawing is incompatible with the rituals of the art world, the glossy catalogs, the opening parties, the reviews. It is a spiritual discipline, it is a Way, it is the Way to where you really live, all ballast thrown overboard.

Your entire orientation undergoes a radical change. Seeing/drawing turns one inward. The "picture" does not matter, but neither is it secondary. It acquires a different function: It becomes a witness to the truth of one's seeing.

6

MEDITATION-
IN-ACTION

I have often been challenged: "Are you justified in claiming seeing/drawing to be meditation?"

I do not doubt that I am justified, for the essence of any authentic form of meditation — whether it is the objectless sitting meditation, the *zazen* of Zen, the repetition of Jesus prayer, or mantra, the concentration on scriptural texts — is to stop the mind's confused obsession with little Me.

In seeing/drawing the entire concentration — for a change — happens to be on what is not-Me, on that rose, that face, that ruin that fills the entire field of consciousness.

It is not only meditation, it is meditation-in-action, by eye and hand in unison. The ninth-century Zen master Daie declared:

"Meditation in a state of activity is a thousand times more profound than that in a state of quietude."

Hui Neng did not, as many of his doctrinaire heirs do, insist on formal *zazen* as the one and only sure way to awakening, to liberation.

I know some — they are few and far between — whose eye is so fully awakened that their artist-within needs neither pencil, brush, cello, nor Steinway. They simply live the artist-within! Their very glance, their slightest touch transmits the fullness of life. They are the salt of the earth.

Is it too personal a confession to say that Claske, for the past thirty-some years my wife, is such a person? I see her contemplating her battery of bird feeders astir with purple finches, chick-

adees, warblers, in a kind of ecstasy, feeding her dozen ring doves, talking to her chickens, her rabbit, and I know this is her meditation. Her constant sensitivity to people in their joys and sufferings has nothing in common with ethical demands or the fulfilling of duties. It is her response to her ever-keener seeing, her inability to just look-at living things.

When I am drawing in the country or in the city, she is not bored for a minute. She is absorbed in her seeing meditation. She does not encroach on my tense attention, she sharpens it, may point mutely at a hawk descending, a homeless person across the street, a little girl playing hopscotch by herself, two old men ambling down a Lower East Side street in talmudic discourse.

"Every poem I write," Joseph Brodsky said in his acceptance speech of the Nobel Prize, "is an immense intensification of what I perceive. Whosoever writes a poem, does so above all because writing poetically is an extraordinary stimulant to one's perception of the world. The one who, in his longing to relive the experience, becomes addicted to it, is a poet." This applies remarkably to seeing/drawing. It is writing a kind of poetry in lines and dots on paper.

"Ah, but what you want us to do is realism," a woman in a workshop opined superciliously.

"Not at all, madam. It is not an 'ism' at all, but if you insist, you may call it radical nonphonyism."

"You say that my poems are poetry," Ryokan, in the seventeenth century mocked. "Well, they are not, and until you understand why they are not, you won't see their poetry." This too applies to drawing: "You say this drawing is splendid. Well, it is not, and until you understand why it is not, you won't see how good it is."

A true drawing is a very private dialogue between the artist-within and some facet of the world around him or her. At the same

time it is the ongoing battle between the self and the Self. If the self defeats the Self, the drawing, however astute, is false, a pseudo-drawing.

A true drawing therefore is never a show-off piece; neither is it ever intended to be a public document, and even less a salable "product," a piece of merchandise. It has as little ulterior motive as breathing.

The slightest trick to mask a sloppy drawing by shading, blackening, or texturing, or by indulging in those multiple overlapping contours that pretend to be a search for form, are mystifications. True drawing demands craftsmanship of the hand, as it does visual intelligence of the eye. Any drawing by Ingres shows both to the highest degree. Cézanne's, Van Gogh's drawings may sometimes be awkward, but they are never affected, never pseudo. Egon Schiele's are neither awkward nor pseudo. Dali's are never awkward, are often almost embarrassingly brilliant. Goya's, Rembrandt's are beyond all such categories.

Michelangelo, I once read, said of El Greco: "He is really a very nice fellow, pity he can't draw very well." Cézanne was in such awe of the craft that he complained in despair of ever mastering it, but he kept working at it until he died. Hokusai at eighty felt he needed another thirty years. . . .

Since in seeing/drawing one "becomes" what one draws, it makes one comparatively harmless. Issa, rendered harmless by his haiku eye, took pity on a fly. While drawing you can't help feeling this compassion with all that is mortal, whether it is the dead

woodchuck on the road, the young bird fallen out of a nest, or the old couple walking their dog. This is what makes seeing/drawing into the equivalent of prayer and meditation.

I am puzzled by what sophisticates mean when they talk about "pure drawing." It must be a formidably esoteric category. I do, however, know, and at a glance, the difference between a true drawing and a false one. Any drawing aiming at effect, or polished to a nice finish and simonized, is likely to be a pseudodrawing. So are those drawings that depend for their interest on extrinsic paraphernalia, whether literary, surrealist, exotic, or esoteric. They may be extraordinarily clever and skillful, make striking posters or illustrations, but as drawings they remain as false as those of a four-year-old are genuine.

Drawing has been described as the art of leaving out. The critical point is, of course, *what* to leave out and why. If I draw an apple tree, it is the life process of that particular tree that must be feelable. Every twig and leaf does not have to clutter the paper, but whatever appears on it should say convincingly: This is neither a poplar, an oak, nor a pear tree! It is not an apple tree, either. It is this particular, unrepeatable apple tree, and no other! This apple tree is my koan!

To solve the koan I must become the koan, be unseparated from it, and this is the "Zen experience" of seeing/drawing: I am in touch with the innermost workings of life in this tree, in myself. For the duration I have become that apple tree.

The next koan may be a young woman's face.

If you break open the cherry tree
where are the blossoms?
Just wait for spring time
and see how they bloom

> *Ikkyu*

7
SOLVING
THE KOAN

We drive into Boulogne-sur-Mer at dusk and find a spot to park on the town's main square, lined with cafés. The tall eighteenth-century buildings stand against a darkening sky. People are strolling in the balmy evening. I open my drawing pad and hesitate. I will have at most ten minutes before it will be pitch-dark! "You are scared," I scold myself. "Don't you trust the reflex arc yet? Let go! What can happen?"

I do let go. The old facades, the thirty or forty strollers, including a noisy drunk, project themselves onto the paper. I may be drawing a crowd, but that crowd consists of thirty times one person, each one related, if only in space and time, to all twenty-

nine others as well as to the architecture of the stage set. It happens in that no-time that I would call "trance," if that word did not have such pretentious overtones. Consciousness narrows down, focuses, sets off the reflex. All else is forgotten. It is an ordeal that in a flash may turn into the exhilaration of total freedom. That crowd is my koan.

Not having a Master, a guru, on hand to approve or disapprove my solution of the koan, I have recourse to a Xerox machine, enlarge the drawing, and find to my delight that the eye-to-hand reflex has registered ever so much more than what I have consciously observed.

In Ostend, on the boardwalk drawing these Three Graces, I suddenly hear my pen scratching on the paper. "Ah! The sound of one hand?" I laughed so loud that the lady in the hat turned around indignantly.

When asked "Where did you draw this?" I can't very well answer: "I didn't draw it, the reflex did." So I mumble whatever comes into my head: "Ah, in Parma, perhaps, or Warwick, New York, or Kamakura."

"How long did it take you?"

"Seventy-two years and about twenty minutes."

"That *is* a lovely drawing!" the man says. I grimace my thank you, but have learned long ago that it probably means no more than: "Nice girl you have drawn. I like her."

I had watched him leafing through the pile of drawings on my table as if it were a telephone directory. Obviously he was as blind

as a bat, but he still had an eye for girls. The girl I drew was his type.

Multitudes of people paint, but few can draw, and far fewer still can see a drawing. For them a drawing is a handmade Polaroid. When they say, "What a lovely drawing," they are apt to mean, "What a lovely girl, or horse, or sailboat," depending on their predeliction for girls, horses, or boats.

The rare ones who do not look-at a drawing as a thing but see it for what it is, a process, a happening, let their eye follow the hand moving across the paper as it precipitated those lines, dots, smears. They do not call "strong" what is merely heavy-handed or crude. They know that a line as thin as a hair, as in an Ingres, a Klimt, a Pascin, has a tensile strength that exceeds a cable's. To see them *seeing* your drawing almost makes your eyes moisten.

True drawings are never mass communication, they are chamber music: no bullhorns, tubas, kettle drums. The lover of chamber music prefers a string quartet to a brass band. The only pretext for exhibiting drawings is the reward of watching one of these exceptional souls seeing them.

ALTHOUGH I AM the opposite of a sightseer — the seeing always again takes precedence over the sights — I can't help being fascinated by Europe's most characteristic sight: It is neither the Place de la Concorde, the Cathedral of Chartres, nor the Piazza San Pietro. It is the bourgeoisie.

America may have its middle class, its upper class, its under class, but Europe has its bourgeoisie. It originated in the French Revolution, when people became burghers, *citoyens*, bourgeois. My great-great-great-grandfather no doubt was proud of being a bourgeois.

To be called a bourgeois, in the course of time, became less than flattering. For over a century, Marxist propaganda denounced the bourgeois as the archenemy of the comrade. Essayists disparage

the bourgeois's mediocrity, his preoccupation with respectability, gross materialism, dull conventionality. Bohemians, artists of all plumage, use the epithet "bourgeois" to express sovereign contempt—as if under his bohemian disguise the "artist" in his

competitive conformism with the latest watchword were not as much a "bourgeois of the soul," as the French put it, as any corner druggist.

The artist-within?

Never!

This European bourgeoisie is not a homogenous caste. By a more or less traditional consensus, it is divided into innumerable subcastes, ranging from the *haut bourgeois* — almost on the verge of nobility — via the *grand bourgeois* and the *run-of-the-mill bourgeois*, to the lowest rung of the bourgeoisie, the *petit bourgeois*. Below the *petit bourgeois* gapes the abyss of the proletariat.

This stratification is not merely a matter of money but of imponderable esoteric factors subsumed as "standing." The run-of-the-mill bourgeois does his utmost to be taken for a *grand bourgeois* by adopting his attributes, from accent to Jaguar and Burberry for the male, to mink hat for the female.

I can't help jotting down their tragicomic attributes, can't help seeing these well-groomed males, these bejeweled females, at this particular moment on their all-too-brief pilgrimage from birth to

death. The plural of human being is an optical illusion, symptomatic of looking-at. Twenty bourgeois, regardless of category, chatting around a café table, are twenty times the one human condition. I hear their chatter as if it were the twittering of sparrows in a tree: the reassuring ritual of hearts still thumping.

Accused of "caricaturing" the *solid bourgeoisie* of the Café de la Poste, the *grand bourgeoisie* of Café Hermitage, the *haute bourgeoisie* of the Caffè Greco, I plead not guilty. I do not caricature these people. They caricature themselves. I see them as I see myself: ephemerals on their brief trip to nowhere. I see their social masks as I see my own, that self-confident, amiable, lighthearted mask, that professional mask of the doctor in his office, the dignified mask of the man on the rostrum, the makeup of the lady in the mink. I see them in their naked vulnerability, for I have drawn naked bodies from life for forty years and have developed an X-ray eye that sees, through all the shenanigans, the poor devils underneath the finery. The pen does not mock, it hallows.

Gustave Courbet said: "Plunk me and my easel down wherever you wish. It is all the same to me." This is the artist-within speaking. He did not chase after "interesting motifs." He knew that the moment the eye opens up, all becomes equally fascinating, equally inspiring, equally pregnant with Meaning.

"You keep harping on Meaning," I hear you scoff. "What do you mean, Meaning?" I really can't verbalize what I mean by Meaning except to repeat again Hui Neng's: "The Meaning of Life is to see." To see what? That life itself is its Meaning! But you'll have to find that out for yourself.

I see it, the Meaning, in clouds gathering and dispersing, in buds bursting open and flowers fading. I see it in leaves, as I see it in faces. I see it in the people on the street, in pigeons in a park, as I see it in the weeds on the roadside. I see it in the mighty political systems collapsing, in photos of once-ruthless dictators dangling from trees, as I see it in the bus: the baby between the man and the woman. Not that it answers your question about Meaning, but neither is it irrelevant to it.

"The mystical of the world is that it exists," Wittgenstein wrote. I could embrace him for having said it, for all that is, is Mystery.

It is this Mystery of sheer existence that impels me to draw. It may seem a useless, childish response, but only to whosoever considers contemplation and prayer to be childish and useless.

The Japanese have two words, *kami-sabi* and *myo*, both almost untranslatable, that refer to the perception of a sacred Presence in all things, in trees, dandelions, and faces. This Presence remains perceptible only as long as it is not verbalized. Just saying: "Oh, isn't that great, isn't that wonderful!" is enough to make the Presence fade away at once.

Kami-sabi demands that total openness by which one escapes from "the grave of custom," as Thoreau called it. It is the profound "ah!" of firsthand seeing. It is the inscape from meaninglessness, it is that state of grace in which all being suddenly reveals the wondrousness of Being.

On the Belgian border where I grew up, crucifixes and madonna shrines still stand on the crossings of country roads. They are like fingers pointing at that which transcends the platitudes of humdrum, everyday life.

An eleventh-century Japanese poem says it sublimely:

What it is that dwelleth here
I know not
but my heart is full of awe
and the tears trickle down.

It is this *kami-sabi*, this *myo*, that makes the hand trace the sacred choreographies of kneeling, of bending backs and necks, of folding hands and lowering eyelids. I see it in the prostrations of Buddhists on the Tibetan border, in the cadences of prayers in basilicas, in the bows and hand claps at Shinto shrines, in the kissing of Saint Peter's bronze toe in Rome, in the brass bands circumambulating Our Lady of Guadelupe, in the staccato series of bows by Hasidim praying in an airport. . . .

I may not believe what they believe, I may not "believe" at all. Seeing firsthand, however, I *know* the sacred. I see it less clearly in the holy objects on altars than in the tabernacles of living flesh becoming transparent, in their bowing, kneeling, making the sign of the cross, mumbling prayers, chanting sutras.

Returned to Warwick from Amsterdam or Kyoto, I draw *kami-sabi* in the tangled weeds behind our house, in the little waterfall a stone's throw to the east, in the people on the beach of the state park five minutes to the south.

Astronauts may wax poetic viewing the earth from outer space, taking pictures of that lovely, touching, fragile little planet. Sitting at the roadside, drawing butterflies on black-eyed Susans, swaying grasses, viewing this earth from inner space, unimpeded by a space

suit, how lovely! Drawing moths and beetles colliding with my desk lamp, how fragile! Seeing my neighbor on his cane dragging himself to the mailbox, how touching. . . .

Bashō saw *kami-sabi* in every blade of grass:

Entering the forest
he moves not the grass
entering the water
he does not make a ripple

Yet nevertheless — it can't be helped — contaminated by the sickness of my time, I entrust my bones again and again to flying contraptions to circle the globe. I can't help belonging to this generation of the restless, the globetrotters, the astronauts, obsessed with seeking, pursuing salvation elsewhere, as if the black-eyed Susans in Provence were more black-eyed than the ones in my backyard. As if being young and American on Main Street were any different from being young in the Grande Rue of a Belgian town. As if to grow old in Kyoto were so different from growing old in Verona or Prague!

Old ones, unenlightened but sane as they are, are often wise enough to sit on benches in parks practicing the Zen precept: "When you sit, sit; when you walk, walk. Just don't wobble."

8

THE SACRED
PRESENCE
AND THE
BODY

Sometimes the sacred Presence, the *kami-sabi*, is shrugged off in order to give it its full weight. When the Emperor of China asked the great Bodhidharma to explain the sacred, the sage shrugged. "Nothing holy, Sire, just vast openness!"

When I first read this, I daydreamed that — with a profound obeisance, of course — I dared to mix in: "Venerable Sir, you say 'nothing holy.' Could that perhaps imply that *all* is sacred, these mountains, rivers, the whole great earth with all that lives on it? And would this not make us guilty of constantly, uninterruptedly committing sacrilege against this sacred earth and its inhabitants, humans included?" Bodhidharma remained silent, but the

emperor muttered: "Sacrilege . . . uninterruptedly . . ." He repeated it a few times.

Then he spat at me: "And what would you, impudent scribbler, do to stop being so uninterruptedly guilty of this sacrilege? Answer, or I'll have your head amputated!"

"Sire," I heard myself say, "what else could I do than to continue what I did today?"

"And what did you do today?" the emperor hissed.

"I drew these humble weeds this morning, Majesty. They are only called weeds: These beings that grow out of the sacred earth must have their sacredness. And this afternoon I drew this old, naked woman, Sire, in her sacred dignity after a long life of bearing, of nurturing children, of boiling rice, scrubbing floors."

"Hm!" grunted the emperor. "And what made you think of this highly original way of interrupting the 'uninterrupted sacrilege,' may I ask?"

"I did not think of anything. I just *saw* the weeds and the old woman. Perhaps, Sire, it was the overflow of the *kokoro*, of the heart. . . . Come to think of it, Sire, I really do not need my head very much."

"Oh well," said the emperor. "Neither do I, so keep it!"

And so, yesterday I was able to see the sun come up in russet glory. I drank my coffee, listened to the murders, shootouts, standoffs, the forecast of rain. The astronaut in me nevertheless persisted in driving to New York to draw humans, according to plan. During the two-hour drive in my old space capsule, it began to drizzle over the ochre fields of New Jersey.

In Greenwich Village the rain came splashing down on Braque-brown brownstones. Crystal bubbles exploded on red, black, and mauve umbrellas. A dull charcoal cloud deck weighed down on the grimy gleam of roofs. People stood sheltering in doorways, staring into the wet dimness. They, the rain, the bubbles, the mirrorings in puddles were orchestrated flawlessly. Everything was exactly where and as it ought to be, in precisely that half-light needed for heartrending beauty.

The sun broke through the dense clouds. On the sidewalk in Little Italy, in front of a leprous "Democratic Club — Private,"

four old men, two gesturing on rickety chairs, the other two stamping around, joined in a passionate debate.

The pen may be mightier than the sword, but it is less mighty than the assault rifle, and so in New York — rain or shine — I draw from my flimsy space capsule. I stop the battered old cocoon at a hydrant, wait until it becomes an almost invisible part of the streetscape. Only then do I start scribbling in the little sketchbook on my knee. Even while catching the conference of retired hitmen, the birthday celebration of San Gennaro in Mulberry Street, this strategy has been crowned with survival. It is my way of coming to grips with that gigantic microcosm that proclaims itself the cultural hub of the world. I draw its cultural manifestations in Chinatown, Little Italy, Lower Broadway, the thieves' market at Cooper Square. I hope there is literally no end to it. Here, seeing/drawing

becomes ever so much more than "creating" pictures, even more than meditation. It is the direct confrontation with life in the raw, in a wild chaos that is beyond all you have ever dreamed of in your philosophies.

"Whosoever has seen the Tao in the morning, can die in the evening without regret," said a Chinese sage. I quote it to encourage myself when drawing the Tao in Chinatown, on the Bowery.

Another one of these ancient Chinese reflected: "The Tao can be shared, it cannot be divided."

And so I share the Tao on Lower Broadway, on Canal Street, as I share it with two ladies, arguing in a snow flurry on the Upper West Side, snowflakes melting around their feet — as if in a Taoist parable.

In the decayed slums of New York, London, Brussels, an ugly beauty survives, a smelly backdrop to human life. It has vanished from the deserts of uptown "urban renewal's" sheer glass, concrete and steel cubes, celebration of big money that rejects all Humanness. The bipeds that err through this wasteland in their dry-cleaned finery avoid meeting one another's eyes for fear of unprovoked assault. There is nothing to draw here.

Then the eye recovers, blots out the glass and steel. The bipeds are humans after all, milling around in their bodies, fat bodies, thin bodies, old and young bodies. My hand starts to move: Life is drawing life again, drawing the human condition. Wherever you draw human beings, you draw the human condition, your own.

Drawing humans on a bench in Greenwich Village, I feel I am catching their images as if they were guppies. Already a new shoal

of guppies swims into my field of vision, scribbles itself onto the paper. Miraculous fish catch!

Drawing these humans, seeing them as if from their center, I am at once in touch with my own center.

It is deep autumn
what kind of life
is my neighbor's
I wonder . . .

". . . and yet, and yet . . ."

I spotted her on Fourteenth Street. She was selling wigs, and to promote her merchandise she wore an outrageous sample on her own head. It made her look like Medusa. But when, as my pen started its scribbling, I caught her eye, I saw how convinced she was that her headgear had transformed her into an irresistible Venus of Milo, with arms and legs emphatically restored. For a second or so, this Venus cast her spell on me. Then, fortunately, the X-ray eye came into action and broke the sorcery. I finished my drawing, equanimity regained.

On Canal Street, in the drizzle, I saw a large old man approaching. I would have taken him for a prominent lawyer, a senator or a company president in his slightly stooped dignity, if he had not worn a faded Hawaiian shirt and carried a plastic bag and a battered little folding table of mottled aluminum under his arm. He set up the folding table, took five little toy dogs out of the plastic bag. He found an abandoned crate and sat down heavily, staring into the drizzle, making the little dogs dance, and waited.

LEAFING THROUGH WHAT I have written here, I stop at the naked tourists in Verona. Neither Eros nor mockery is involved, merely the result of some forty years of drawing from life, in which the eye slowly but surely evolved into the X-ray eye that pierces all attempts at camouflage.

What this X-ray eye sees are not "nudes" but the naked bodies we are when we take off our coverings, and that it is not the naked

body but its packaging, however minimal, that performs the magic trickery of promising erotic bliss forever. Without the packaging, how naked that body, how unsettling in its defenselessness, its relentless stages of aging. Seeing this does not annul passion. It enriches passion with empathy, with the tenderness, the reverence that enables one to love.

From time to time I am accused of "sketching."

"Oh, I do like that sketch of your Venus," or "the one of the Grand Canal!"

I plead not guilty: I do not sketch, I draw.

There is a difference in principle. A sketch is the product of looking-at, a cerebral conceptualization. The smart-aleck intellect chooses a few striking characteristics. The tree, sketched, becomes a vertical stick with thinner sticks welded or glued to it. A forest sketched is a multitude of such stick diagrams overlapping.

A drawing is the result of seeing. When I draw the tree, I am faced with a mystery. I must enter into this mystery or fail. Whatever I draw confronts me with the mystery of Being.

9

ART AND
AWAKENING

The lightning-fast drawings of Venice by Turner, those of people by Rembrandt, far from being sketches, are wonderful drawings, done at high velocity.

They are more: They span the chasm between Western art and that of the Far East. For Rembrandt and Turner complied intuitively with what had been the ideal of art in China ever since the fifth century, when Hsie Ho wrote his manual on painting. According to Hsie Ho, the artist must identify so radically with the *ch'i*, the movement of life that animates all things in nature, that its spiritual rhythms resonate in his work and create those linear rhythms of unbroken fluidity that mirror the mysterious reality of the universe. In East or West, this is the essence, in Bach as in Rembrandt and Turner.

Kafka writes about a carpenter's hammering a table together, "as if this hammering were all that matters, and yet at the same time a Nothing."

What else is seeing/drawing but this passionate hammering that is at once all that matters and a Nothing!

And what does it matter whether this Nothing is labeled with the honorific "art" by the enthroned authorities of the moment?

I stand by my own definitions: "Art is what opens up the clogged pores of perception, what transmits the pulse of life," or else: "Art is that which despite all gives hope." I not only jotted this down, I carved it into a wall. Hope of what? Hope of being human enough to do something wholeheartedly, without any ulterior motive — however anachronistic this may seem in a culture where "normalcy" consists in striving for fame, profits, and selling more of "the latest," "the newest," whether in "art" or anything else.

ONE DAY IT was raining so hard that I took shelter in the Museum of Modern Art and found myself amidst dense clusters of mortals gaping at the gigantic canvases canonized by power and prestige, certified as masterpieces of the latest avant-garde-but-one.

How dated these jumbos already looked! How curiously out of touch was their "modernity" with all the vexing realities of our postmodern world! They seemed as unrelated to life as-it-is, as the academic salon jumbos of a hundred years ago. They were still proclaiming business as usual, still boasting that originality for originality's sake that Jorge Luis Borges deplored as a "contemporary, impoverishing myth." All they seemed to prove was that the more inflated the narcissistic ego, the larger the acreage of canvas it needs to "express itself" in its incoherent originality.

Rembrandt, too, once painted a jumbo canvas. But his tour de force demonstrates almost superhuman skill, insight, sensitivity, substance. Moreover, the *Night Watch* belongs to his early period. The great works of his maturity, the profundity of his later portraits, of that self-portrait in the Frick, are, however modest their size, as shattering as Beethoven's last string quartets.

In his drawings Rembrandt proves beyond all argument how independent the inner dimension, inner space, is from size. Each one of his postcard-size Holland landscapes is a precious lesson: Those few square inches suffice to embrace the fathomless spaces of the universe.

There is no large no small
Infinity lies before my eyes
Seng-T'san, sixth century

It is almost funny to remember how in the years when I was still on the exhibition merry-go-round, I was always worried: Was what I was showing really "original" enough? Was it really "of my time"? Was it "strong" enough?

It was of course not "original" enough, for original means, as I found out later, to be in harmony with the Origins; I was not "of my time" but of its follies and fads. And as to "strength": Is not to be afraid of tenderness the ultimate weakness?

Simone Weil wrote: "A work of art has a maker, and yet a perfect work of art is also anonymous, as if it intimated the anonymity of the art of the Divine. And so does the beauty of the world offer proof of God, who is at once personal and im-personal and neither the one nor the other."

"Art is not what expresses personality, but what overcomes it," is T. S. Eliot's maxim. His and Simone Weil's are curiously congruent. Listening to a Bach fugue, to his *Magnificat*, I do not hear a Mister Bach "expressing himself," I hear that which transcends Bach and us. I hear what no theology has ever proven: that — under whatever name — God must exist. I hear proof that the Experiment Man has not failed: This music too was made by one of us humans! We, humans, can do more than build missiles and produce junk food for body and mind! We have painted as Piero della Francesca, written elegies as Rilke, requiems as Verdi, Mozart, Schubert, Palestrina!

SOMETIMES WHEN DRAWING, I have the feeling that what I am actually doing is no more, no less than breathing in and breathing out: I breathe the world in, and breathe the drawing out. The pen does the rest.

If this drawing, for instance, should remind you of Alfredo's Pizzeria, I am not surprised. Yet to me, while drawing, it was just what I breathed in, then breathed out, any resemblance to Alfredo's being purely coincidental.

A while ago, breathing this landscape in and out — such things are most likely to happen where one grew up, where seeing started — I felt that these trees, these crows were not out there, in front of me, but inside of me.

Then you draw an inner landscape that looms up from the formless, colorless Ground of Being, it transposes itself briefly,

inexorably, into form, into these trees and birds and into the soft haze of gray that envelops the trees, the crows, and the one who draws. There was no being "creative" at all! It was that moment of grace in which you are touched by the mysterious process of unceasing Creation, participating in it.

Not long thereafter, the news was so full of terrifying rumors of war, of the number of planes and tanks on our side and on theirs, that I fled into an orchard near our house and started to draw an apple tree.

Drawing that tree and the couple of lovers that came walking through the orchard did not neutralize the terror. Still, I became quiet, filled with gratitude that, come what may, I was still allowed to sit here with my drawing pad, breathing it in, breathing it out.

I got home and I saw that I had scribbled underneath "The Splendor of the World has no Why." I was perplexed. The Splendor of the World . . . no Why . . . It kept resonating in me. Where did it come from?

Only now, as I am writing this, I remember Angelus Silesius and his rose without Why. . . .

A few weeks later, in the wintry gloom of another war that — as wars will do — came inexorably, I looked out of the window and saw our white rabbit, fancying itself a snow hare. Coal-black eye afire with delight, it was jumping crazy capers in the falling snow, white on white!

Again, "Splendor of the World" flashed through me, and I mused that it is this Splendor — without Why — that had kept me drawing through most of this century of agony.

It must be a response born with me, as if it were a little tune I have to sing, even as a dirge, when the Splendor is eclipsed by all the violence, amidst the squalor, the insanity that — God knows — has its Why.

Our most "original" sin against life must be that, day after day, we forget the unfathomable mystery of being here — for a little while of being here at all — ultimate mystery of sheer existence. . . . Or perhaps it is neither "original" nor "sin." Perhaps it is no more than a structural flaw that makes for our blind stupidity that, coupled with the delusions of our self-enamored ego, believes itself to be far more real, far more sensitive to the joys and pains of living than any other ego. As if this little ego were the only valid observation post of all things between heaven and earth! What else could account for the folly, cruelty, greed, fanaticism, racism, and all the other symptoms of our horrendous "normalcy" that denies life?

When for a split second the blinders fall off, there is the Splendor! Nothing is commonplace. All is brimming with the Splendor — without Why.

ONE DAY A monk spoke bitterly to the Buddha about the unbearable sorrows of the world. The Buddha remained silent. Then a faint smile appeared on his face.

He pointed at the earth between his feet, and said: "On this earth I have attained awakening."

Splendor of the World . . . no Why.

EPILOGUE

Could seeing/drawing be a small victory of sorts, that of the human eye over the horrific "normalcy" caused by our conditioned nonseeing? Could it be the liberation from our addiction to looking-at?

While seeing/drawing, I seem to retrieve my connectedness with the three-hundred-thousand-year-old roots of the artist-within-me, which is none other than the Specifically Human-within-me.

BUTSUGEN, in the eleventh century, said:

"You monks, straining day after day to understand what Zen might be, are barking up the wrong tree! What you can't seem to

see is that *all* is beyond understanding, not just one thing or many things, but every single thing is fundamentally beyond our understanding. The Really Real in its Suchness is beyond our understanding. Just *see* it in this light."

Seeing it in this light, I see/draw, I draw what is beyond my understanding, That Which Matters, the Really Real, is right before my eyes!

It is not hidden!

Seeing/drawing is more than making pictures: It is witnessing to this seeing, it is touching the Meaning.

One day I saw that the sun was round
Ever since I have been the happiest man on earth!

The artist-within is the one who sees and witnesses to this seeing: whether in the great ones, in Bach, Rembrandt, Piero della Francesca, Rilke, or in the lesser ones, even the very little ones. . . .

Wherever I go
I meet him
He is no other
than myself
yet
I am not he.
　　　　　Dosan

What shall I leave behind
empty skies
fields
grasses
dandelions
birds swooping
faces, faces
each one veiled
each one mirroring
the Face of faces.

Farewell, farewell
hands waving in mist . . .

Issa

Dr. Frederick Franck's drawings and paintings are part of the permanent collections of more than twenty museums throughout the world, including the Museum of Modern Art, the Whitney, and the Tokyo National Museum. He holds degrees in medicine, dentistry, and fine arts. Author of a score of books, including *The Zen of Seeing* (Vintage, 1973), *Echoes from the Bottomless Well* (Random House, 1985), *The Book of Angelus Silesius* (Random House, 1978), *Life Drawing Life* (Great Ocean, 1989), *The Buddha Eye* (Crossroad, 1989), *To Be Human Against All Odds* (Asian Humanities Press, 1991), *Days with Albert Schweitzer* (Holt, 1960; new edition: Lyons & Burford, 1992), and *A Little Compendium on That Which Matters* (St. Martin's Press, 1993). Dr. Franck lives in Warwick, N.Y., where he restored an eighteenth century mill ruin into an "oasis of inwardness," Pacem in Terris, Peace on Earth.

"This book is a crystalline gem, the quintessence of the Taoist wisdom of creativity in action. Frederick Franck shows us once again how simple it is to rediscover the artist-within. This beloved sage-teacher, a Renaissance Man for all seasons and for all the world, has created another marvel for us to treasure forever!"
— Chungliang Al Huang, founder, Living Tao Foundation, author of *Quantum Soup* and co-author of *Thinking Body, Dancing Mind*